A SHEPHERD'S
JOURNEY

A SHEPHERD'S
JOURNEY

A narrative and challenging mission of the Church of Christ in our world as experienced by an Anglican priest.

Ven. Dr. Stephen Adédòtun Adésànyà, Ph.D

Foreword: The Rt. Rev. John Richard Packer

Copyright © 2012 by Ven. Dr. Stephen Adédòtun Adésànyà, Ph.D.

Library of Congress Control Number: 2012900649
ISBN: Softcover   978-1-4691-5106-9
             Ebook   978-1-4691-5107-6

The right of Stephen Adédòtun Adésànyà to be identified as the author of this book has been asserted by him in accordance with the Copyright, Designs and Patents Act 1988.

Some of the people mentioned in the stories in this book are fictional. All the stories are based on real situations.

Also by Stephen Adédòtun Adésànyà
1. The Caring God   - 1998
2. The Sexes under God   - 2000
3. A Useful Visit   - 2001
4. A New Understanding   - 2003
5. Marriage is a Nest not a Net - 2005
6. Your Manifestation of Purpose - 2007

All Scripture quotations, unless otherwise indicated are taken from the Holy Bible; New International Version (NIV). Copyright acknowledgement (where not already indicated under References)

All rights reserved. No part of this book may be reproduced or transmitted in any form or by any means, electronic or mechanical, including photocopying, recording, or by any information storage and retrieval system, without permission in writing from the copyright owner.

This book was printed in the United States of America.

To order additional copies of this book, contact:
Xlibris Corporation
0-800-644-6988
www.xlibrispublishing.co.uk
Orders@xlibrispublishing.co.uk
303390

Contents

1. Imusin—The land of the Ackee tree..15
2. Into My Beloved Yugoslavia..42
3. In the Church Of Nigeria..52
4. The Social Concern..66
5. In the Church of England 90
6. The Business of God's Mission 114
7. Stephen in Teesdale 129
8. A Shy Young Man 147
9. The Dead Rocked the Boat 157
10. Mission Implications 166
11. The Anglican Covenant..183

Definition Of Terms..201
References 205

Dedication

This book is dedicated to fellow pilgrims on this road of life.

Author's Note

I am privileged to work with Zarah Smith and Kathy Cooper at Xlibris Publishing, London, U. K and appreciate their wonderful suggestions and help in shaping this book. I started writing this book three years ago, when I was confronted by certain situations already discussed in this book. During the period concerned, I looked through Libraries for a book that will help me but found none hence I decided to write one. I had not set out to stir controversy, but to find a way to reduce the heating within the polity and to examine individual and collective contributions to the divisions that has distracted the Anglican Communion in both the Global south and north. Any part of the world may have issues with any of my assumptions and this may indicate how different others perceive our actions. I had highlighted some aspects of the culture and how they have affected the Church in general, and that culture and reason rather than alienate us from the heart of Christ can draw us together in love and into Christ. We need to have a constant positive relationship with every individual despite the condition of that person. We are faced with a more fertile ground for evangelism today. A challenge of our Christian journey is to love others without conditions, walking along with them, discussing how the Gospel can benefit all. I hope that this book will bring a fresh dimension into the challenging situations we may find ourselves and an insight on how it was dealt with. My prayer is for all who are struggling with the controls of their lives, that the almighty God through His Son, Jesus Christ may continue to give us wisdom that we may always trust and obey His word in the Scriptures.

A Shepherd's Journey

A narrative and challenging mission of the Church of Christ in our world as experienced by an Anglican priest.

Foreword

When Stephen Adesanya came to the Tees Valley in 2009 we knew that both he and we were developing an exciting and challenging experiment. Stephen brought a deep spirituality, a passion for mission, and academic rigour to this deeply rural area of the Pennines. As he tells us, some warned that this was too far away, physically and mentally, from ethnic London. For those with ears to hear Stephen has brought new perspectives on Christianity and encouragement in faith. In 'A Shepherd's Journey', Stephen draws on his wide experience in Nigeria, former Yugoslavia and England. He is not afraid to be critical, of racism, prejudice and violence of deed and word. This goes for both Europe and Africa, and Stephen's unique variety of experience means he is ideally placed to comment on many of the issues with which the Anglican Communion wrestles today. Through it all the warmth and determination of Stephen's character shine through. There is deep affection here as well as realistic questioning. Anyone who reads this book with an open mind and heart will find themselves drawn nearer to the heart of God with deepened faith and understanding of our contemporary Church and world.

+John Packer
Diocese of Ripon and Leeds
2012

Acknowledgements

Much of my ministry of the past twenty-plus years has been assisted by support from various organisations, and the ideas generated in this book have been part of what has nurtured me. I wish to mention the Federal Government of Nigeria; The Government of S.F.R. of Yugoslavia; and Evangel Theology Faculty, Osijek, Croatia, (as they were at the time of their scholarship); from whom I have received scholarships and grants received from Iskra Delta Computers, Ljubljana, Slovenia and other bodies and persons in Nigeria, Croatia and England. I feel privileged to study under Prof. Rev. Peter Kuzmich, Rev. Bob Beard and appreciate their wonderful suggestions for my early ministry. I wish to thank all my friends especially Provost Kola Fasanmoye, Ven Titus Abolaji for their eternal optimism and for all their help and Otunba Abiodun Adesoye for his tireless support. The value of their contributions and suggestions cannot be overstated. I thank Major–Gen. & Mrs Timothy Babatunde Ogundeko for their belief in my work and care for my wellbeing. Useful comments on drafts of some of the chapters have been received from Bp. Ayodele Awosoga, Bp. John Packer, Archdeacon Janet Henderson, Andrew & Christine Bracewell, Rev Alec Harding, Ven. Dr. 'dapo & 'Toyin Sotonwa and Prof. Gerald Blake, and for sharing their critical eyes and logical minds with me. Su Graves who gives me administrative support assisted with the word-processing of some of the chapters of this book and for her suggestions. I am grateful to Bogdan Repe, Prof. 'Segun Odunuga, Milan Milutinovich, Jeff & Carol Lynn for their friendship. I thank all my teaching colleagues and students at Archbishop Vining College of Theology, Akure for the inspiration and fellowship. I am fortunate to have been guided by the insights of Pa & Mrs J.E.O. Olagookun, Oladotun Odunuga, Peter Hughes, Keith Watson, Penny Sunderland, R. Modupe Olowoyo, June Armstrong and Mrs

Adenike Omoyajowo. I appreciate their labour and contributions. I am grateful to Adekunle Daodu, Segun Demuren, Phillip Arundel, Nathaniel Aina, Elizabeth & Nike Okunowo, Emmanuel Adekoya-Ogo Oluwa, Ven. J. Fowowe, Rev. Stanley Haworth, Rev Peter & Shirley Lind-Jackson, Rev. fr. Malcolm Johnson, Barbara Packer, Rev. Mark Williams, Rev. fr. Angus Galbraith, Rev. Roy Dorey, Prof. Adeleke Adeeko, Rev. Neil McKinnon, Dr. Sue Proctor, Bp. Olubayo Obijole, Bp. Christopher Chessun, Bp. James Bell and Prince Bayo Otulana for their invaluable contribution. I could not have written this book without the encouragement of my family and other friends especially Mrs. Mary Shepherd. I owe them a lot. Thanks are due to my brethren in the Churches and communities, the Wardens, Secretaries, Vergers, Organists, Choir and all the Parish Church Councillors with whom I have worked so far for their love and all their help. I am indebted to Bishop John Packer for reading the first draft, his suggestions, and encouragements and for writing the Foreword. I would like to thank my parents and Prof. Mira Kapetanov for their love and care, Bishops A.S.O. Olowoyo, J. A. Omoyajowo, Dayo Oladunjoye, Olubayo Sowale, and Ayodele Awosoga for their trust and character which reflects Christ Jesus.

Venerable Stephen Adédọtun Adésànyà, Ph.D.
Barnard Castle.
2012

Chapter One

Imusin—The land of the Ackee tree

Ijebu-Imusin consists of many villages and hamlets with a flourishing market at the centre of the town. Kabiyesi, The Oloko of Ijebu-Imusin is the paramount ruler of the town, even though there are other kings such as the Magusen in Itamarun, the Oyebola of Igbaga and the Obelu of Esure. The Ijebu-Imusin Annual Rally which traditionally holds from the month of August is a major tourist attraction for the entire town, which involves age-group carnival parades, during which time most children and adults are indulged with gifts and fun. One aspect of the season is that it helps the development of the town. For indigenes and friends who attend from far and near, they enjoy the celebrations into the early hours of the following day. The Isin tree (Ackee) stands in the market square as the symbol of the town beckoning as a place of refuge. Ijebu-Imusin is unique for the cooperation that exists among the indigenes of the town as the sons and daughters ensure that whatever is good in other places are obtained such as the post-office, community Bank, town Hall, etc. This ancient Ackee tree (Ackee translates into 'Isin' in Yoruba language.) has been identified as the grave marker which Obanta, the third ruler of Ijebu, planted on the grave of his son who died on his way to Ijebu-Ode where he was crowned king. This tree is today in the centre of Ijebu Imusin, in the market square which though is fully operational every five days from dawn until nightfall, yet the market flourishes daily. According to Brochure 2000, Ijebu believe that their ancestors migrated from an area of Sudan called Waddai, that also in itself means a parallel migration wave like other Yoruba who believe they came to present day Yorubaland through Oduduwa. The Ijebu are united under the leadership of their paramount ruler and King, Oba Alaayeluwa,

The Awujale of Ijebuland. That is why the unfolding drama of the Sudan in the past forty years or so has been a matter of concern. There are many peoples from different areas of the sub-Sahara Africa that lay claim to have migrated from Sudan, most especially from the southern Sudan city of Juba many centuries ago due to internecine wars which forced some of these people into the tropical rain forest area which is not profitable for both arable farming and cattle rearing. The tropical rain forests of West Africa was known many years ago as the white man's grave, but what was not said at that time is that the anopheles mosquitoes that help the spread of the parasite causing malaria fever is as dangerous to the health and wellbeing of white men as they are for black people. It is assumed that the vast majority of death in the sub-Sahara Africa is malaria caused, and there are still poverty induced malaria fever causing serious health hazards to the populace. It was therefore a joyous occasion watching on television the people cast their votes after many years of war between the Arab north and the people of southern Sudan, which led to a declaration of independence. Even though, it remains to be seen how the wounds of the oil rich state of Abyei shall be healed in the long run, it is hopeful that the effects of such a state of war would not be left to fester as was the case between India and Pakistan, or North and South Korea. This time Nigeria and Cameroun have something positive to share with the world, how they shared their northern boundaries a little over fifty years ago and recently shared between themselves their southern and oil-rich Bakassi peninsular without resort to war. This is clearly the duty of the United Nations to ensure that people are not left in a state of war and by ensuring that the wishes of the inhabitants of this area are respected. There are evidences to support the fact of migration from Sudan such as the Sudanese tribal mark which, is variously used in Yorubaland. The three vertical marks on both cheeks used to be the traditional identity in Ijebu, which they also share with the Tigrians and ancient Axumites. The Ijebu also share funeral rites, and the Agemo cult with the Egyptians, the Nubians and Puntite people and they share many cultural ethos with these people. Ijebu Imusin is blessed with human and mineral resources such as Oil Sands. According to Russ 1924 and Reyment 1965, the Imeri area of Ijebu-Imusin just off the Lagos-Benin expressway falls within the Oil sands belt in the Nigeria sector of the Dahomey basin.

The Early Years

The wonders of what I have experienced, seen and heard in the past has not robbed me of the lessons learnt from my parents in infancy, which were of course very deep and enduring. I grew up in a polygamous family, and I enjoyed relatively my moments but have not got the privilege to compare it with any other life since I have only got one. I grew up along with my siblings having an evening meal all seated on mats spread on the ground in the courtyard, and it was always a plus when the moon was up, giving light to everyone, otherwise our wick-lamp gave enough light. The enemy then were the ants—be they flying or marching black ants, which would bite whenever we squatted on their paths, or threatened their marching. I had started my primary education by an act of God's providence. At that time my mother had to go to the farm and as I would be a greater burden if she had to strap me to her back carrying loads of cassava tubers from the farm and it might also endanger me if any fell on my head. I was often left to roam the corridor and play on the School field close to my father's house till the school broke up for the day. One day, a mentally-challenged man walked up the road, and took off with my dress. I had earlier removed the dress, while using it to catch grass-hoppers. When my mother heard from my senior brother that a mad man went off with my dress, at the close of school on that day, she went after the man. She found the mad-man sitting under the legendary Ackee tree, the tree that gave my town its name, pleading for the release of my dress. The mad man opened his calabash pot and brought out my dress which by then was stained with palm oil. With gladness my mother returned home, washed the dress and was happy to see me wearing the dress again on my way to school the following day. With the benefit of hindsight, what could make a woman beg for a soiled dress from a madman? After this incident, the teacher found it hard to allow me to play by myself outside the classrooms, except during the break time, therefore she made sure I was always sitting underneath her table whenever the classes were on. This kind teacher was the queen of the King, Kabiyesi Oba Jaiyeola, The Oloko of Ijebu Imusin as at 1963. Anytime I remember this story, I wonder how many dresses I had at that time of my life, and what was going on in my mother's mind as she was pleading with the mad-man to show mercy. Towards the end of the academic year, the teacher was giving the primary one pupils the promotion test, and all was silent, no one in the class knew the answer to many of her questions, but I requested for the chance to give the answers. To the surprise of everyone in the class I provided the correct answers to the questions from beneath her table. At that point in 1963, I was promoted from beneath the teacher's table to be found a place within the body of the class as a bonafide primary one pupil at St. Mary's Anglican School, Ijebu Imusin in 1963. I salute the courage of Mr O my primary three class teacher in 1965. An incident in class that left me with a wound did not allow the teachers to administer corporal punishment on me till I left primary School. My father threatened to bring in the Police to examine the situation if he does not receive an official apology. Therefore, all my father's children were nicknamed 'Kam Salem's children' by the headteacher and this was because the name of the Inspector General of Police at that time was Kam Salem. However, the following year I got into problem with a class four teacher for late payment of Harvest dues, and since I could not be punished like other children in School, this teacher who is a friend of my family decided to pull my ears. As she pulled my ears, in pain I stepped back and stumble at the mobile black-board. The board fell down on me and I developed headache. The teacher told me on taking me to the head-teacher's office for first-aid, not to confess that she pulled my ears, but jokingly called me an 'element' which was translated by the class to 'elementie'. This was how my first nickname was developed. At that time, there was no electricity at Ijebu-Imusin. The first time I experienced electricity was when I went with my mother to Lagos in 1968. Electricity came to my home town, Ijebu Imusin in 1975. I spent my infanthood following my mother wherever her business took her—to the farm, river or market, and learning from a tender age how to carry loads delicately balanced on my head. Looking back to those days, it must have been very hard; walking bare-footed on the sun scorched stony roads. In those days, I was only allowed to wear shoes on the days of Christmas, New Year, Easter and Harvest festival on my way to and from the church. As one that attended a church owned school, I was a member of the choir until well into my third year in the secondary school at St Anthony's, a Roman Catholic grammar school at Ijebu Imusin. My parents were Christians and I normally would be by their side on our way to church, or must have robed as a chorister before their arrival in Church.

Claudius and Adebisi

Prince Claudius Adefuye and Comfort Adebisi Adesanya—my parents have since died. They were great assets and counsellors, and they related with me as great friends do. The transition of my parents, step-mother, mother and later mother-in-law into the nearer presence of God was very stressful. Within six months of each other they moved from here to the hereafter, but my father died the youngest, but much earlier in time. Over five hundred people attended the funeral of my father at St. Mary's church, Ijebu Imusin when he died at the age of seventy-eight years. My mother died at the age of eighty-three years old, after a brief illness. Claudius and Comfort my parents, 'Bimpe my step-mother and Anike—my mother in law were very much loved and respected in our communities, as reflected in the way the people paid tributes during the celebration of their lives at the receptions following their funerals. My parents were missed by all who knew them and they left behind an enduring legacy. Prince Claudius Adesanya was a man without malice; tolerant, tender-hearted and clear-minded. A courageous man who faced life with all that it brought. His death and that of my mother, respectively were tests of faith for me in different ways, but I was comforted in the fact of the Bible's teachings on the issue of resurrection, and I look forward to see them again in the new world, the heaven that God has promised us as Christians; as they now rest in the Lord (Rev.21.1-4). Surely, I had a good spiritual start in life. My parents began morning and evening devotion in the house in 1974, just before I passed out of the secondary school, but by this time I was becoming restless, not wanting to hear anything of the Gospel and trying to assert my independence of mind. My friends then were also imbibing the beliefs of Karl Marx, which was quite a pressure on me, and was however fashionable among the youth as a response to agitation for liberation in Southern Africa. This was meaningfully propagated from the lyrics of Bob Marley in his reggae music. As a teenager, I was happy to escape to the then Socialist Federal Republic of Yugoslavia on a Federal Government of Nigeria scholarship. This helped me to exercise my new found freedom and secularity. From 1977 until 1991, I studied Electrical and Electronics engineering, and later Christian Theology and graduated with first class degrees. I lived in present day Serbia, Croatia, Slovenia, and visited a host of other countries which include Austria, France, Belgium, Libya, Germany, Holland, Belgium, Egypt, Montenegro, Bosnia, Israel, Sierra-Leone, Liberia, Malta, Greece, Bulgaria, Holland, Germany, Italy, USA and the UK, before I returned to Nigeria. My Christian life was virtually extinct and not seen in my Yugoslav life from 1977 as the communists were in power, and I joined my peers to do what we most enjoyed such as disco dancing, partying and travelling, but in all these I was flourishing with my education. I left home with high hopes to strike gold, and it was with great determination to succeed in life that I left Ikeja International Airport, Lagos, Nigeria in 1977 on the flight to Belgrade, Yugoslavia. I have in the past, after my initial reluctance to attend classes in my first year in secondary school turned a new leaf, and in an effort to adjust through life indulged in reading and I would rather say, much reading. I was reading every available piece of paper in sight, nearly all the James Hadley Chase novels, and the writings of William Shakespeare, Oliver Goldsmith, Jane Austin and anything in print, be it a newspaper or an advert. I must have indulged in this to suppress some of the complexities that I have passed through in life. My situation in life was not helped by the fact that I was the first child of my father's second wife. I could imagine my father struggling to cater for a wife with four children—Adebisi, Ademolu, Kehinde and Idowu, when for any reason he took on my mother, whose first marriage ended in a divorce on the grounds of infertility. Her first husband had sent her packing when there was no conception in their seven years of marriage. The hostility was brazen and glaring from some of my father's immediate family, and I lived with this until much later by which time God has broadened my horizon. I was later to have two surviving brothers and a sister—Adesoji, Adedoja, and Olumide—from my mother, with my father having a total of ten surviving children. My father's first wife later had Opeoluwa, and Mosunmola. In Nigeria generally, and among the Yoruba in South-West Nigeria in particular, there are three types of marriage: customary and Islamic, which permit polygamy, and ordinance, which is legally monogamous. If a man is married under ordinance he cannot legally take a second wife but permitted under Islamic or customary law. In fact, marital laws are not respected by many Nigerians and it is common for a man married under ordinance to marry other wives according to tradition. All married women may therefore be living in a potential polygamy, despite the marriage vows of their husbands. Adesanya 1997 in a study, Nigerian husbands were asked whether they would prefer having a second wife or a girlfriend. The finding revealed that fifty per cent (50%) of the husbands prefer having a second wife; twenty-five per cent (25%) prefer having girlfriends while another twenty-five per cent (25%) will try neither. In the same study Adesanya asked the wives, the difference is more pronounced. Sixty per cent of the wives (60%) selected a second wife as their choice, while thirty per cent (30%) of the wives preferred to make no choice at all. Those wives rejecting the choice warned that "A girl friend may later become a second wife or that either a second wife or a girlfriend may come with concerns for the matrimonial home". When choosing a second wife, the reasons often adduced is that it is better and cheaper to have a second wife whom you can trust than to maintain a girl-friend that is unreliable, but Christians prefer marital chastity.

The SANTOS Years

Some incidents stood out from the time when I was twelve years old and I was admitted into Saint Anthony's grammar school, Ijebu-Imusin (also known as Santos or SAGS), of a frail physique but my parents were determined to see that I have a proper education. I have my maternal uncle to thank for this, who saw to it that I got admission forms to enter secondary school. At that time my father felt that he was not able to send two children to the grammar school at the same time as, a senior brother from my step mother was also eligible. When I was twelve I started in the secondary school. My first day at school was hilarious as it was interesting. Right by the gate of St. Anthony's Grammar School, popularly known locally as 'Santos' were the senior boys. Those with a year's seniority were especially desperate to impress it upon us that we were 'junior boys just enrolled'. At every little interval, the senior boys would enter our classroom and challenge us as to why there was so much noise in our classroom, showing us that we were yet untutored. In our first three days at school, the senior students took turns to give us different forms of corporal punishment for noise making, speaking vernacular, loitering, dropping litter or for improper dressing. Their usual order to us were in form of 'stand up, raise up your hands and close your eyes', or to give us a portion of the grass field to cut, and sometimes a portion on the wild grass. As soon as one of them realised we have had enough, we would be pardoned and at the next moment another one would punish us again. At a point during break time but I did not realise break was over, I was coming in from the pit latrine when I passed by a class and indeed they were making some noise. So I entered the class, asked them to 'stand up, raise up your hands and close your eyes'. I punished them before I realised they were not my classmates. Worse still, only the senior boys could punish the juniors and this was only my fourth day in the Grammar school—putting my learning into action. When I realised what had happened, I could not go back there out of fear and they served out their punishment until a teacher came to their rescue. After about two weeks one of them recognised me and dragged me to his class, and I confessed, they beat me up mercilessly and made me serve further punishments, cutting long tracts of the field. The spate of punishments that followed from the set of about seventy boys in this senior class led me at a particular point to contemplate putting an end to my miserable life. It was as if seventy hungry wolves descended on a small rat, there was no one I felt I could run to, and waking up in the morning for school was very challenging. I spent each day at school serving different forms of punishment, and by the third day of the week, my only white school uniform would have turned dark brown from dirt and sweat, labouring in the sun cutting grass or weeding or picking stones depending on the disposition of the senior boy who allocated the punishment. The self-induced punishment my mistake caused me was quite enormous. I was running away from school for about two weeks and hiding in every available shed or bush on the way to school and only leaving my hiding place after school hours. When it was time to return home as I would join others walking home as if I have been present with them at school. One day, I was disgusted by it all, I recollected an event from one of the literature novels I had read and I looked for a tree stump which served as a table in the forest, sharpened my cutlass and after delicately placing my left arm on the stump, tried to give myself a cut. This however did not result in any serious bleeding, as the laceration caused an inflammation of the damaged muscles, and the veins swelled. My desperation did not allow me to feel the pain, feeling disappointed with myself I got myself a razor blade from a nearby corner shop and returned to the tree stump in the forest. I slashed my arm with the blade, sweating profusely, having previously worked myself up in a frenzy of physical exercises but again God spared my life. I was late in returning home that day and evoked a lot of sympathy from my parents who neither realised that I was not attending school nor knew that it was a self-inflicted injury, as they took good care of me as good and loving parents do. As I was not in the boarding house, one day one of the senior boys requested that I should help him buy some stamps and some edible items from the town, which I did, but I could not recognise the senior boy the following day. After some time I ate the edibles and started spending some of the money which I should have returned to the senior boy with the purchase. Another week gone by, this senior boy recognised me and took me into his class for punishment for late submission of purchased items, and I promised to bring them to him the following day, however he gave me some punishment and after classes that day, he followed me home. As he was reporting the incident to my father upstairs in the sitting room I bolted away not thinking about how I would survive. I knew that my father was popular and remaining in our town would be useless, so I ran to my late maternal grandmother's village with the intention of staying in grandma's house, since my grandmother was four years dead and her house was uninhabited. I got there to realise that the door was locked, and the fear of being found loitering by the night vigilantes which might spell death as they might assume I was a thief was very frightening. Therefore I ran about two miles into the dense jungle and was sleeping rough, under the shades of cocoyam leaves and living raw in the forest for about three months. The white school uniform in which I made my escape from home was at about this time torn into shreds and has turned very dirty. Every day, I would move from tree to tree finding what to eat and would lay down just before darkness made movement virtually impossible. I listened most of the night as different types of animals made their way across my new abode. One night, a python came and coiled round my foot, and as she probably found it warm and enjoyable decided to tarry a while, but I was petrified to say the least and having known the implications of the serpent feeling I was not hospitable enough, endured it. Sometimes, I would cry when I woke in the morning—angry that I was conscious, that I had to live another day, angry that I was alive, hateful of the mere thought of ever returning to school and dreading what might be awaiting me from family, bullying school mates, and the repercussion for absence from school for such a long time. One day, I remembered that in my father's house there was warm food and shelter, and feeling sad and dejected, I decided to fetch something in my grand-mother's hut in the village, a box of matches with which to light a fire and roast for myself a tuber of yam. However, not realising that at that moment my father's search party were within the house of one of my Aunts in the village. They were lamenting my disappearance and I was trying to get a box of matches from the outer kitchen of the same house. Suddenly, I found myself surrounded and captured, handed over to my sorrowful father, who at that time was at the centre of his feuding wives who blamed him for my absence from home. I thought my father would severely punish me and members of his search party were telling him in my presence to tie my limbs and make me pay dearly for all the stress into which I have put all the family, it was very scary for me. But my father kept his counsel and said nothing as he brought me back home on his white bicycle, a distance of about five miles. When we got home, my father asked that I be fed and then asked me to have a bath and a change of clothes. Whatever led to my father's decision, he went to his grave twenty-eight years later without talking about it. The following day, my father personally returned me to school, after a detailed discussion with the senior student involved and a plea with the school principal. That approach of my father remained a life changing experience for me, as it also helped me understand the teachings of the Gospel narrative of the parable of the prodigal son when I had the grace to read or listen. Another incident which I could never forget happened, in 1972, when there was a football match between my alma mater—Saint Anthony's Grammar School (SAGS) and Ijebu Ode grammar school (IOGS) which is the premier grammar school in my province. That day I was in the third year in the grammar school when I understood that SAGS and IOGS were about to meet in a football competition. When I was young, sport was not encouraged and it was seen as something truants do by our parents, as the belief then was that decent children must always be found studying and not playing away their life. The English saying that *'all work and no play make Jack a dull boy'* was unheard of at that time. Prior to this match, I had not watched any football match between SAGS and any other school team and I decided to see for myself all the school heroes at play such as bros Oye and for what IOGS players like Yomi who doubles as a star player for the regional academicals could do with my school heroes. I sneaked away to Ijebu Ode grammar school in our school bus, a distance of seven and a half kilometres, chanting and yelling support for the SAGS team. It was very good, and it was quite an amazing game. My school heroes gave a wonderful performance, they were simply great, but the IOGS won the game no thanks to Yomi who scored the lone goal notoriously nodding the ball into the net with just a few minutes to the end of the match. On return to the school, and eventually arriving home, I needed to tell my parents where I was, but it was unimaginable that a decent boy from my generation would tell his parents he had gone to watch a football match after school as far away as seven kilometres at Ijebu Ode. Therefore, I told a lie that I thought could save me from punishment. I told my parents that on my way home, I met a white garment prophet who delayed me with prophesy about the length of my years of life. My parents were naturally disturbed; my mother knew what I was up to and took it with some disdain and wondered aloud to me why I needed to say that to save myself for coming late from school. But daddy was determined to search for this man of God for further explanations, for he was worried. My father took me on his white Raleigh bicycle and pedalled from village to village in search of the man, but the entire search ended in futility as the man did not exist in the first instance. As my father carried me from village to village, I was very sorrowful with the knowledge of what my insincerity was causing him, but my mother had the last laugh as she ensured I was duly punished for my offence. Whenever I played truant, my mother would ensure that she woke me when everyone had gone to bed, and then I would serve my punishment, without disturbing the peace of the night as alerting others by any form of noise could only have multiplied my punishment. She was a determined woman, and whenever she looked at her children even in a crowd, that child should understand the non-verbal message or else a punishment would be served later in the evening for disobedience. I hate to think now of the pain and anxiety I put them through looking back at the naughty boy that I was. Whenever I was in the presence of the opposite sex, no matter what age, I would feel their overbearing presence and overwhelmed, partly due to my experience of siblings dynamics, suspicious of their intentions and could only look at the ground, but with boys or the older men I was a talking gong. My school work began to suffer, but I picked up academically when I was promoted to primary six in the top ten among the group of seventy pupils. I tried to play the fool or sometimes self-sacrificial, giving myself to others, yet it did not stop the bullying from family members. For many years after my graduation, I was happier in the company of friends rather than in my extended family. I tried to hide my anger from my traducers with the pretext that I was a shy person, and dared not risk getting close to many people. This helped me hide my disturbances from others who might pry into my predicament, and despite all my academic success, it was not easy finding joy as I grew up. I just loved to be left alone. When I was admitted at St. Anthony's Grammar School, Ijebu-Imusin, Nigeria, between 1970 and 1974, I was privileged to have been taught by some wonderful characters such as Revd. Fr. Donahue (Biology), Revd. Fr. Curran (Physics and Math) and Miss Smith (English) among others. These Roman Catholic priests and Nuns could have been Irish and Miss Smith might be from either England or Scotland. They have left Britain to be in the mosquito infested tropical rain forest of south western Nigeria to make my life and other children's lives better. Like Esther who decided that *"if I perish, I perish"* many of them came to Africa not for commerce or colonial expansion, but to give the African child a chance to be educated and motivated. Fr. Donohue and Miss Smith eventually died in a road accident in Nigeria and during my college days, some other catholic priests from my school also died in road accidents. The issue was that they left Britain of their time to come into Nigeria of my youth, where they were only able to have hurricane lamp and where the vast majority of the motorable roads were dusty, no running water, mosquito infested environment and taking regular supplies of anti-malaria tablets weekly; they were no doubt an important minority. Their situations were more precarious than mine for their zeal and faith in their God. Not much changed in the family as the years went by, but there was much love and goodness in my life from my parents, and my mother's family who gave me opportunities to do that which most children could only dream of.

My father's Farm Project

I was not familiar to using cutlasses and machete as I was not brought up in a farming family. The only time I could recollect my father on a farm ended in catastrophe. My father out of wishful thinking to farm when I was nine years old asked for a plot of land from one of his close relatives, Pa Ogundeko and he leased to him a piece of land to farm. On the first day when the land was to be cleared, some farm hands were recruited for the task and it was a major day in the history of our family as activities were at a peak in preparing and ensuring that all the essential implements needed for farming were ready. By 5.30am, my father had woken every member of the family, breakfast was prepared and we were ready for a thirty minutes' walk to the farm led by Pa Ogundeko who showed my father the boundaries of the land. After that came another day designated for gathering the dried trees that were cut down during our earlier visit to the place and another day for planting the cassava stems, yam and cocoyam tubers. On our fourth day working on this farm, we actually spent more time hearing the stories my father had to tell us while eating our breakfast than doing the actual work of farming, as my father rested his back against a palm tree. One day after many months of neither attending to the farm nor talking about it, my father came home from Ijebu Ode where he had his shop, and decreed that the following morning everyone must be prepared for the farm for some harvesting. Whatever prompted this order from above, I could not imagine it. But surely, it was to save the crops. We were disappointed by the spectacle that confronted us on the farm. The farm was overgrown and there was no trace of a farm being there in recent years. My father tried to harvest a few struggling cassava plants but nothing useful was found. There was nothing of cassava, cocoyam or yams for us to harvest.

The Virgin Teacher

One incident that stood out for me when I was growing up and for which I measured my ignorance as a growing young chap, happened when I finished secondary education, at which time I was a virgin. I had made one or two attempts due to peer pressure to befriend a girl in the past, but each time I would be intimidated by the girl looking at me expecting me to cough out the essential words. I was so shy in the presence of the opposite gender. One day, as a teaching assistant in a primary school, I was in the company of three other friends and they were boasting of their popularity with the ladies, and how one girl had given two of them a venereal disease. In the particular school, two of my friends have girl friends among the staff, and unfortunately for me one asked if I was dating a particular girl whom they felt was friendly with me. No, I said; my girlfriend had recently been snatched by another man, I blurted out. How did this happen and who was the chap who snatched my girlfriend? One of them was out to avenge for me the indignity meted to me. I gave my story, how much I loved this girl and gave all the attention to her, and because of my love for her I would be with her for most times whenever the situation arose. One simple question, they chorused, did I woo her and did she agree to be my girlfriend? I kept quiet because I had neither asked her to be my girlfriend nor had she heard anything from me. I was just assuming that because we became very close the deed was done. I was stupid and I lost her to the person who asked her. The discussion with my friends disturbed me for some time that I decided to chat with the first girl that would allow me to smile with her, and I had a particular girl in mind. I invited her to my father's house and we danced on our feet and with our clothes intact, but I made sure some of my friends came around before she left, to secure my honour among friends that indeed I was not spineless, and I could talk to a girl even though despite all my pretentions, I did not have any intimate relationship with this girl. I had not seen this particular lady since then (for surely she might be a grandma by now, as I had become a grand-father also), but I was seventeen years old then, when this happened.

My First Job Offers

My first job search on leaving secondary school in 1974 came at a huge personal cost for me. I would leave Lagos Island where I lived with one of my maternal uncles by bus to Palm Grove, then walked several miles from Palm Grove bus—stop to Aswani textile mills in Isolo, Lagos because of my limited financial means. I was sure that I must have made this trip up to eight or more times on different occasions as it was my only reliable hope of securing a job in Lagos, while dropping off my application, checking up for developments, interviewing and follow-up before I was eventually employed. Another uncle, Laide, who occupied a top government position made this contact possible after many visits to his office. One day, he called in his office messenger who owns a part-time tailoring outfit to make two trousers and two shirts for me. This was a great privilege as it was my very first pair of trousers in life apart from my final year school uniform. This was in 1974 and the Oshodi expressway was under construction at that time, which meant that as I walked along the route I would be covered with brown-reddish dust from head to toes by the time I arrived at the Aswani Textile Mill or from the firm back to Lagos Island. I could recollect how everyone on the Lagos Island bound bus was gaping at me as I returned home to Lagos Island on my first day to Aswani in search for job, as I was a pitiable sight. For more than ten days I was going to Aswani Textiles with the hope of securing the job, after all I was well connected. On a Monday, as it was traditional for most Lagosians of my ilk, I woke up at 4.30am to complete my morning chores and by 5.10am I was inside a bus from Lagos Island to Palm Grove bus stop courtesy of the few coins that another Uncle has given to assist with my transportation. I was to complement my bus ride with an hour walk from Palm groove. I resumed work with my newly sewn and ironed trouser and shirt and I also had the effrontery to put on a tie that was knotted for me by a friend. This friend made sure that I had with me a nylon sheet that would cover up my precious suit through the walk along the dusty road to prevent either dust or rain from spoiling my day. The personnel manager who was doing my uncle a favour showed me to a small table. Barely thirty minutes after my eight o'clock resumption, the personnel manager sent for me and apologised to have put me through all the stress of employment procedures. With a show of regret, he told me that he had noticed on my application form that I was underage, that I was not employable. It was illegal to employ someone under seventeen to work in the factory under the labour laws. I was gobsmacked, crest—fallen and I walked through the factory gates like a mourner unto the street. I had just been employed for the first time in my life and sacked for being underage. This experience led me to return to my parents' home at Ijebu-Imusin. Later I applied to the Local Schools Board to become an auxiliary teacher and I was given a job after turning seventeen at Omu-Ijebu, where I was a teacher not much older than many of the pupils that I was teaching. After school hours, I would go with some of my pupils to the stream and to play in market places as teenagers of my age do. One day, we were caught playing pranks after one of us kicked the ball into the evening market square, and as we tried to retrieve our ball, one of the children assisting their mothers recognised me. This boy greeted me respectfully and I can recollect the awe on the face of the mother who realised that even though tiny and playful, yet I was a teacher.

The Young Man's Suffering

I was sure that my parents would be quite over the top if not over the moon when I was born. My growth would not have been different from many other children of my time, but what I lost from my frail physique, had been compensated by my ability to speak boldly. I could keep quiet and be alone, and introverted for a long time, yet I could debate issues for hours without resting, depending on the company. I could run around endlessly as I was sometimes restless, throwing tantrums at friends twice my strength or older as I grew up. Right from my youth, my parents who were miles away from medical sciences, viewed the pain radiating from the upper left chamber of my chest cavity and concluded it must be pneumonia, but medicine proved it in later years to be something else. And just like the stomach disorder that traumatised me for some time before my arrival in Europe it was diagnosed as something else. At a point in my life I suffered acute abdominal pain, and pain killers were of little help. My father asked me to return home and took me to a herbal healer. Early in the morning one day, my father made me get ready as I sat on his bicycle bar to travel about four miles to the native doctor. The man asked my father to say whatever his problems might be into the hand holding the money and dropping it into a bowl of sand which he did. At this time I had just returned home after my aborted search for job in Lagos, and it was a few months after finishing my secondary education. I sensed that this was the medicine man's way of collecting his consultation fees. After the man had recited some incantations which sounded more of poetry to me, he looked up as if assessing me and declared to my father that the cause of my stomach ache was that I had just impregnated a light complexioned lady and that my father must force me to confess. This I knew to be far from the truth because as at that time I had no girl friend at all and I had no girl close to me for the past two years, more so as at that time I was a virgin. My father implored me and when I could not confess to anything, gave me some knocks on my head which was quite hard for me to bear because up till that time there was nothing I said that my father would not believe. Later some white garment prophets in the Nigerian indigenous churches were to instruct me not to take gari or any cassava food because they erroneously believed it was the cause of my stomach ache. When the pain would not cease they told my father, that probably I was still sleeping with someone with whom I should never have had an affair. These false prophets and traditionalists were of the opinion that acute abdominal pain was the punishment or a curse on a young man having illicit sexual affairs with a married woman. But I had no such relationships and if I had died in Nigeria at that time, it would have become a shameful end. This falsehood and other experiences helped make up my mind when others were leaving the Anglican Church for one reason or the other into other Church groups. I had barely arrived Serbia when my appendix burst, and I thank God that the facilities in Novi Sad were able to cope with the situation.

The Wedding

During my stay in Serbia, I was always in Nigeria during school-break because my father compelled me to visit Nigeria annually. He did not want me to lose touch with my roots no matter the situation. As I grew older, I was conscious of life's goals and I felt that I was ready to be married at the age of twenty-five. Right from my teenage years, I had a proto-type of what Mrs Right should be, and even though I have gone the opposite of this utopia of mine many times in the past as I chose girlfriends, I had certain pre-requisites as to what I needed on a permanent basis. In 1982 before I celebrated my twenty-fifth birthday anniversary, I met Olubukunola nee Ogunbawo a-k-a Buki who was visiting her colleague close to my family home at Ijebu Imusin. I was able to chat with her for two days in Nigeria before I returned to Belgrade in Serbia, but within ten days of our first encounter and despite it being a long distance relationship, we got engaged and we got married that year. After my engagement to Buki, we were always in each other's company whenever possible. We were never intimidated by the presence of people around us, and never shy in each other's company. Wherever we were, people wondered how we could hold on to each other's hands while walking the streets. To many Nigerians at that time, it was novel, unacceptable and people were wondering if that was part of my training overseas. Maybe yes. It is strange to the Yoruba culture for couples to hold hands or hug in the public. I was creating a cultural problem but I had always loved to be touched on the cheek, and to feel wanted even as a child, a luxury that I rarely got in those days. We were happy hugging each other publicly until the torrents of complaints started pouring in to me and to my parents and it was becoming problematic going out together for all the sarcastic looks that came our way. Even though we claimed to manage the situation, yet we became more cautious in our romance. Sometimes, Buki would touch my hands, while trying to chat with me or to ask a question. If I may ask; why did she behave that way? What exactly do females want to achieve? This had been a golden question that confounds men. Surely, men do touch a lady for a purpose, and the men knew where they stood at that point. I may wonder why males and females touch each other, for a so called innocent touch tells stories of sub-conscious motives. Men behave like giants yet they want to be treated like a doting child with all the care and loving attention from the wife. Would it be part of the reason why a man would cherish putting his head on his partner's lap and be comforted? All of us can never forget the role of romance in marital happiness. We were married with a lavish reception after the church service at St. Peter's, Imosan with family and friends mostly in attendance. As I had spent most of my recent years abroad, I was only able to invite a handful of friends, most of whom I met during the national youth service corps year. As a young man recently married to a working nurse, some of my friends made a lot of jokes about me, as to what my experience would be on a rainy night when my wife was on night shift, as it was rare for her not to be away a week in a month on the night shift. I knew that would be the case before I married her as I went into the marriage with the knowledge of her vocational demand. Since I knew I would not be inviting many friends, I got myself two cartons of beer and two barbequed chickens prepared in a sauce and the accompanying well cooked rice and fried ripe plantain with a crate of Coca-Cola to go with it. After the party I was left with a surplus of half the crate of minerals and a carton of beer. My father on one hand wanted me to make provisions for an army of people that he was inviting and believed that I should also invite as many people as possible. I did not have such a fund to lavish but I also did not believe in this approach. I was looking forward to getting my new family a piece of land to build something moderate and also establish an enterprise but my father was only looking at having a large party to celebrate my wedding. Yes. There was a huge party largely organised by my parents, in-laws and siblings, but I invited the few that I knew as friends. Buki gave me two beautiful sons—Adeolu and Adedotun, and I became less nomadic. She gradually helped me return to the church, by her subtle encouragements and approach. In 1982, I returned to Nigeria to serve the National Youth Corps year and to spend time with my family after my marriage and to enjoy family life, and this was made easier by my employment at Tomol Nigeria Ltd, as one of the management team of a company involved with turn-key laboratory projects in many places of Nigeria. But ill-health cut short my stay in Nigeria as I was told at a point at the University College Hospital, Ibadan (UCH) by medical consultants in Nigeria that I needed to return to Europe before I die prematurely. I was becoming a pitiable sight to my parents who were seeing me gradually wasting away, and in a state of constant shock due to palpitations. During this delicate time of my life, an Uncle, a retired major-general in the Nigerian army assisted me greatly both financially and with counselling support. Major–General Timothy Babatunde Ogundeko and his loving wife, Patience were a presence of God in my life, and I thank God who enabled them give me such a massive help when I needed it most. I was constantly going back to Yugoslavia for medical help for most of 1984-85 when it became obvious that it was better for me to stay in Europe. But in 1991 I returned to Nigeria, because of the nostalgia for home. This is because there are many aspects of the Nigerian life that anyone would always enjoy. There are many difficulties in Nigeria but it is a place to be, to enjoy the laughter or the anger of the people, the Nigerian people are a happy people.

The Oil for Our Relationships

Yet, it was not all smiles on my wedding day; no thanks to the part played by some members of my extended family. One of them had led some others into a calculated and well planned error and a particular part of my extended family tried desperately to disorganise the wedding. A section of my relatives tried desperately to smear my name that day. My wedding day events left a deep agonising scar on my psyche not because of my bride but because of what was done to me by close relatives. For some time, I hung to the emotional turmoil of my youth, avoiding those family members that I perceived disliked me. But when I reached out to them like the Biblical Joseph, I overcame the ill-feelings, and forgave the real and perceived ills; this made me a happier person. After all Christ Jesus says *forgive and you shall be forgiven*. We have a wonderful God that is able to deal with the situations of our lives. Either we are abused or ill-treated; God can deal with the situations. Whenever we allow the LORD to touch our wounds, there will be a newness of lives, not only for us but also for others around us and for our relationships and this is my experience. There is a big lesson for us in Mark 15.1-5 which teaches us to avoid sinful reactions. We must never hang on to hurtful feelings, but forgive by letting people off the hook even when no apology has been received. At the foot of the cross, with people yelling, the scorn, pain and the indignity of the Cross, Jesus found strength and said: Luke 23.34 '*Father, forgive them for they do not know what they are doing*'. Jesus in Matthew 6. 14-15 says: '*If you forgive men when they sin against you, your heavenly Father will also forgive you*'. It is only when we learn to forgive, that we shall grow in character and humility.

Robbers on the prowl

After my sojourn in the western world for over a decade, I grew home sick and decided to return home to my sub-Sahara African nation of Nigeria in 1991, where I could sun-bathe all the year round. No! Did I refer to Nigeria as a nation? Nigeria, a country of many nationalities, has been trying to forge nationhood since it was amalgamated into a country in 1914 and since the 1960 independence from Britain. Recent events in the country have challenged the foundation on which we grow our nationhood, but we are optimistic that though tribe and tongue may differ, in a true federal state of Nigeria we stand. In my home town where I built my house, I was subjected to armed robbery attacks ten times and in one particular year before I left the house, it was ransacked three times. At the tenth time, not only was the house maliciously damaged, our items such as ceilings were broken, personal items stolen, window blinds and the electrical fittings and wirings were pulled off the walls and carted away. I wept bitterly the last time I was there, realising what hatred and cruelty man could inflict on another person, and the people whom I grew up to believe were my kin and kith could inflict on me and my family. This probably is because hoodlums felt that I am a rich man, and they inflicted unimaginable agony and pain on my immediate family. The robbers once pointed a gun to the head of my son from whom they demanded to know where I kept valuables in the house. After the eighth attack on my home I left Ijebu Imusin for good, as I knew the lives of me and my family were not safe, as they thought I must be richer than they met each time they struck. Two other attacks were made on my residence subsequently. Yet, I could not get the police to do anything; they were simply not ready for my type of client. On one occasion, despite the cruelty of the robbers on the tenants in the house, even when one of them pointed out who had assaulted her, I could not get the police to arrest the brigand. This robber was an 'untouchable', and I got mad so as to put my neck on the line as I confronted this robber in his house and requested his family to warn him when all attempts through the police echelons to deal with the situation failed. I knew I was playing with fire, but I was also tired of living under the strain, experiencing the torture from robbers and hooligans. Though there were ugly incidents as senior police officers were being jailed in other parts of the country for various offences including armed robbery, aiding and abetting, corruption etc. At its simplest, the presence of immigrants is an indication that the problems they were escaping from are beyond them, not because they were cowards but because they flee from a superior power. It was fantastic fighting for your rights especially when you are not just kicking your foot against the Alps or Kilimanjaro mountain but knowing the structure you were up against and the resources available to do that. The welfare system, liberty and social justice which many western nations take for granted are not even available as a privilege in many places and any effort to ask questions might determine if you are to remain alive or not. I went into the offensive and even went the full length to confront the identified robber and criminal. I went from one police authority to the next level and nearly the full length of the police administration in my state to report the matter, but alas, no one, not even the identified suspect was arrested. At the time they came to my house and met my immediate family, the situation of the family in the hands of these villains was better imagined than narrated. Unfortunately, that day the money I had in the house was only two hundred Naira which was equivalent to a meagre eighty pence which was in my cassock pocket. It was unimaginable what would have befallen me if I had been in the house when they struck, because they would assume I was not cooperating with them and the result might have been fatal. This happened on the eve of my installation as a canon of the Cathedral while I was at the rehearsal in church and my family had gathered to felicitate with me and be part of the service the following day. On the day of my installation as canon of the Cathedral Church of Our Saviour, in Ijebu Diocese, an event when the drums were rolled out, followed with dining, yet anyone who watched me closely would realise that I was more of a sleep-walker than the actual celebrant of the day. I was eager to escape the crowd to find a lonely place where I could quietly rest my body on a bed. Admittedly the day of my installation as Canon was the day after the eighth armed robbery attack on my house, when my family was badly and emotionally tortured, and I could not catch an hour of sleep as I kept guard over my family throughout the night in the open with only the moon and the singing mosquitoes who kept company with me. I sat outside throughout the night watching but this was about bolting the door when the robbers have actually spent their time and left. That was the last time I slept in that house and I became a refugee in my country because subsequent visits of the robbers to my house left me financially and emotionally traumatised. Later a land mark robbery happened close to my house, as a man was preparing to bury his mother. According to the narratives of those who were the vigilantes that night, the family had locked all their doors ready for a good night's sleep and the robbers banged on the door asking the occupants to open the door and the burglary-proof iron-wrought gate for them. In Nigeria from the 1976 onwards till the year 2011, houses are built to provide own source of water and electricity, security and often must maintain the road leading to your house. It is like everyone is a government of its own. It is now normal for Nigerian homes to look like a fortress but more a prison with fortified walls complete with iron gates and windows. The residents of the house refused and as one of the robbers put a pistol through a broken window brandishing it to threaten them to open the door and gate. A courageous lady snatched the gun from the robber's hand. They threatened further, and pleaded and bargained to no avail. The robbers then burnt the cars in the vicinity of the house to show their seriousness and threatened to burn down the house with the occupants inside it. In order to pacify them, this lady threw a stone through the window into the bush and pretended that the gun had been thrown out of the house. The robbers then went on a wild goose chase till nearly day-break and as they were burning part of the house either to kill the residents in an act of arson or threat, help arrived from the neighbourhood vigilante who had mustered some courage to act. The robbers eventually fled with enormous damage done to the house. The courageous lady turned out to be a top police officer from another part of the country that had come to take part in the funeral rites of her relative. When day broke, she found that the gun in question was a police service pistol allocated to the head of the district police of my area. A lot of noises were made but it simply confirmed that the robbers were protected from the high places by those paid to maintain order in the society. Some members of the community and the King, Kabiyesi, Oba Oloko of

Ijebu Imusin enjoined me to remain in the house because it is mine. I knew that this would be foolhardy, as I would still be carried out of my house if I allowed myself to be killed by those who felt that I was rich enough to be plundered. However, I had always loved Ijebu-Imusin, since my youth it is a place where God often relieves me of much distress and I was not ready for anyone to dispossess me of my heritage. More so, not having a home in Ijebu-Imusin for an indigene is like not having anything in this world. The question was, why has the situation degenerated to this level of lawlessness? What recruitment process allowed us to employ potential armed robbers into police and security formations? Why does an individual has to provide his own family deep-well, electricity, transportation and security? When you grow up in such a constant state of insecurity, you do not know where to find peace, as the government seems only concerned about the welfare of the very powerful and their officials. The Church properties are not immune to this tragedy, but the fear for lives may have encouraged the Church officials to tread softly. The insecurity is confounded by assassinations and political thuggery within the polity. This is the core of the problem. Many of the responses that the Government has taken in recent years have been ad-hoc agenda to deal with situations that are generally on the ground. Such instances include Government responses to issues of national insecurity by a Joint Task Force instead of making sure that every part of the country and all residents wherever they are in the country feel safe and secure in Nigeria. There is a need for the reorganisation and retraining for security outfits in the country, and assistance may be invited and received from those with the required expertise. By the selective security provided by the special task force instead of equipping and training the police to provide adequate security to everyone anywhere within the country will not be addressing the deeper issue. A generation of Nigerians born from 1970 onwards are now in danger of not knowing what peace and security means, or the enjoyment of three square meals daily. The coming generation will like to learn about character, citizenship, loyalty and dedication to duty and not the trail of embezzlement of Government properties, the bribery on the roads to police officers who man roadblocks and that after their education, there is a light at the end of the tunnel job wise. The coming generations will like to learn about love, care and loyal service to our country, and want the leadership of their country to show this by their example of leadership. Why is it impossible for the multi-nationals and the big business to insist on doing business with governments that take care of their people and provide guaranteed minimum security to all residents?

The Guidance of Children

I had taken a cue from my parents who never tried to fit the children into a box as far as career path is concerned. Adeolu opted for his educational programme based on the score from his GCE examination result. It was a challenge for me when Adedotun decided to study at the University what Adeolu was studying, but apart from guidance I decided it was in his interest to support him. It has been my passion to give my children a good start in life, without over-pampering them. I would have loved for one of them to read my engineering, theology or counselling psychology books but that may be a tall dream. The duo are exceptionally talented children, and now with postgraduate degrees. I pray they shall continue to forge ahead with learning and good character to benefit families and nations. The naming ceremony of Ololade my first grandchild as it is traditional among the Yoruba was on the 7th day after his birth, and full of joy, I danced from dusk till dawn. I could say that Buki and I were the happiest persons living when with Adeolu and his wife Kehinde, we took to the dance floor. Children are to be what God has created them to be, not meant to be replicas of their parents or pushed into a mould designed by them. The Biblical example of the lives of Saul and Jonathan can be our guide in this approach. King Saul wanted his son to be king after him, while he looked at David as a good commanding officer, yet Jonathan befriended David as a friend whom he loved. David began to thrive among the people, even though Saul became suspicious of him, but we noticed that Jonathan remained a loyal friend to David. The summary of the story is that King Saul refused to get acquainted with and be fit for the role God expected of him yet he stubbornly intended to mould the life of his son. He lost the crown, his son and his life in a battle which catapulted David into the throne of Israel. The approach of parents, difficult as it may be for some people, shall be that of continuous guidance but above all supporting the children with prayers as they take the decisions of their lives.

Back to Lagos

After one academic year as a pupil teacher and because of the special programme of the Government to train teachers, I was admitted into Methodist Teacher Training College (MTTC), Sagamu in 1975 to obtain the minimum qualification of a grade-two teachers' qualification. But it was never my dream to be a teacher. Meanwhile, Mr. Gbolade Onanaike, my uncle and other close relatives such as Onafujabi a.k.a the manager and Duro Banjo assisted in securing another job in Lagos. Three weeks into my stay at the Methodist Teacher Training College, Sagamu, I got an offer at the Federal Surveys department in Lagos as an assistant technical officer in training, the position of a trainee lithographer for three years. However, two years into the training programme in 1977, I was offered a scholarship to study Electrical/Electronic Technology in Yugoslavia by the Obasanjo led federal military government of Nigeria.

Chapter Two

Into My Beloved Yugoslavia

It was a pleasure living in the present day Republics of Serbia, Slovenia and Croatia from 1977. Actually joy and happiness were scarce until I got a scholarship to Yugoslavia, where I met with true joy and friendship without any harassment from anyone. It was an experience of freedom and liberty. I was able to chat along with others and I began to see myself not as a first child of my father's second wife, or from a family position. From this point in my life I saw myself as Stephen Adedotun Adesanya, a person born to shine and succeed, a child loved by my parents and God. In the cold winter evening of December 1977, I arrived at Novi-Sad via Belgrade having earlier been entertained at a reception organised for those of us, who were scholarship students from Nigeria on the specially chartered flight in Malta, where we had a stop-over. The meal in Malta appeared quite delicious but my African background saw it as a chicken not well cooked, therefore I stayed hungry, hoping to have a meal at my destination. On arrival in Belgrade we were transported by coach to Novi-Sad in the autonomous province of Vojvodina within Serbia, and took cover under the blankets in the room that was allocated to me. The following day, I heard a bell ringing, and every time I tried to get out of bed the chilly air drove me back, yet I was desperately hungry. This struggle went on until the door was forced open at a point by someone and he asked if I had eaten and I said I was hungry and he announced that lunch was nearly over, yet the time to me appeared like six o'clock in the morning. That was my first lesson in Europe, never to judge the time of any day by the appearance of the sun. I was determined to make the best of my time in Yugoslavia, as I saw it as a once in a life time opportunity, always recollecting the quote of my father which he wanted all his children to remember at all times: *'my son, always remember the son of whom you are'*, or Proverbs 1.10 *'my son if sinners entice you, do not give in to them'*. I wanted to live up to the unique meaning of my name—Adedotun—as I wanted to excel in life and never to disappoint either myself or those who wished me success.

Sojourn in Novi-Sad, Serbia

In 1977 when I arrived in Yugoslavia there were only a few dark skinned people in the Socialist Republic of Serbia, and a negligible few in the autonomous province of Vojvodina and the provincial headquarters of Novi Sad and whenever I ventured into the villages with my friends the reception was extraordinary. What started for me as an embarrassment became something I looked forward to and enjoyed as a celebrity. Many people in the villages would come out on to the streets to see and touch a black man. They called me a 'Black man' and that in Serbian is 'Crnac', and it did not bother me, and of course this was the time before political correctness became generally popular in Europe. The questions the people asked ranged from, "where are you from?" "Do you live in houses like ours in Africa? " Why are you black and we are white?", "Do you enjoy sex?" they would point at a lady and ask if I would be willing to have sex with her. They would touch or hold me and tried to see if my colour would rub off and then sometimes the children would want to know if it were true that Africans have tails. Sometimes, I wondered what to say, when questions such as these came from the adults or elderly people. As a young man in Eastern Europe I grew up to be defensive and in an environment that made me always conscious that I was different to people among whom I sojourned. At first the questions that the Serbians asked were felt to be embarrassing, malicious and hurtful, but I eventually realised that they meant no harm. They were straight talkers and you always knew where they stood, which was not a distant position to that of sub-Saharan Africans. I was always eager to go on vacations so during school break and sometimes even on weekends I found myself always in one place or another, in Nigeria, Italy,

Greece, Turkey, Hungary, Austria, Bulgaria, France, Switzerland Holland and sometimes the USA, but like a migrating bird I always wanted to go back to Serbia, which I recognised as home. At that time, finance was not any challenge as I was a scholarship student and I enjoyed student fares. Therefore, even when I left Novi Sad for Belgrade and later to Ljubljana in Slovenia and Osijek in Croatia, I found time to go to remote villages where I enjoyed my celebrity status with the population getting the opportunity to touch me and ask questions over meals and drinks. The people of Serbia, Croatia, and Slovenia, Bosnia and Herzegovina, Macedonians and the people of Montenegro among whom I interacted were a hospitable people and lovely to be with. Within my first six months in Yugoslavia I have been hospitalised twice. As I was recovering from my burst appendix I imagined how lucky I was to be in Yugoslavia at that time. As I laid on the bed having just returned from the emergency surgery, I was wondering what would have happened if my appendix had busted before I arrived Europe. It would have been fatal. I enjoyed the movement to the emergency department as the siren howled and every other vehicle gave us safe passage, it was like my moment of glory. The urgent evacuation from my hostel to the hospital reminded me of the title of a book I loved to quote 'Triumphant Gate' by Erich Maria Remarque who says *'When you are living, no one cares for you but you are highly important when you are dead'*. This is my own translation as the book that I read was written in Serbo-Croatian language, the present day languages of the Serbs and the Croats. As I laid sick I thank God for all the help and care of my friends, both Yugoslavs and Nigerians. Two years later I had a massive stroke for five months, lying in a position for long hours before being turned over, in a manner reminiscent of preventing a barbeque from burning. Mystery still envelopes what occurred to me in January 1980 when I was paralysed in my left limbs in Novi-Sad, Serbia. I ended up in the care of a teaching hospital even though I was the previous night hale and hearty watching the world amateur boxing competition held in Belgrade, Yugoslavia and actively supporting a Nigerian pugilist who eventually won a gold medal. I was in this state of health being transferred from one hospital to the other, my blood pressure according to physicians throughout the ordeal remained normal, a mere 117/80 yet I was less than twenty-three years old. I was conscious of the agony my parents would be suffering, not being able to hear from me, they would have been praying frantically, and I felt a pity for them. Would I die in this cold foreign land without the privilege of saying goodbye to my friends? Would anyone of my relatives ever be able to trace my grave? Would I meet with the God my father talked about so much, and if yes would he be as merciful unto me as my father often described him to be? I was always delighted to see Prof. Mirjana Kapetanov who stood by me through thick and thin, giving all the moral support, and at a time arranged for one of my friends—Borka—whom she knew was a special friend to me to accompany her on the long trip to the hospital from Novi Sad, Serbia to the University Hospital in Ljubljana, Slovenia. I was one of the three Nigerians in her Mathematics class and we confounded the class by our gifts in the mathematical sciences. Abiodun, Kola and myself were sometimes the envy of fellow students as we often step up to proffer solutions to difficult situations in class. Prof. Kapetanov, my disciplinarian mathematics professor was very sympathetic and would bring me provisions, and I was often more worried for the disappointment and anxiety that I was causing her than for my health. After many tests through various hospitals and across the towns and teaching hospitals in modern day Serbia and Slovenia, I was alerted to the fact that I might not get my health back. There was a 90 per cent chance I would end up on the cold table in the morgue and that if I survived, it shall be a 10 per cent chance that I would be wheel-chair bound for the rest of my life. All this time I knew my parents were praying especially for the fact that they had not heard from me, they must have intensified their intercession on my behalf. The five uninterrupted months I spent in the three different hospitals in Novi-Sad, Belgrade and Ljubljana were full of anxiety and expectations. During my ordeal I nearly lost hope of meeting my friends and family especially Leke, my bosom friend and eventually my best man and telling him of my dreams and how I survived this traumatic period of my life. Sometimes, I wondered about life after death and what happens after the grave. There was so much going between Leke and I after we both left secondary school, so much as to be sustained during this period by the aspirations which we both shared. We also played pranks together and shared dreams, as we shared similar background in many respects. Leke's mother and my father were blood relatives. When I could manage it, I could almost seem to hear Prof Kapetanov giving lectures in class from my hospital bed, and when I played the truant, heard her say, S T E P H E N—A D E S A N Y A, for she would call out my names in full whenever I have played truancy, and this was always to be expected. After the fifth month on the hospital bed, immobile as I was, and hardly audible, one evening I was thinking of what would happen if I had to meet with Christ on the judgement throne. I did not believe in him at that time, I dozed off and dreamt and I felt so hot in my sleep that I sat upright on my hospital bed and realised how much better my arm was and as I attempted to get out of my bed to the loo by myself, the nurses crowded round and prevented me from getting up. I was sweating profusely. Everyone believed I was about to die, or that superstitiously, I might soon die, so they were alarmed. To God be the glory! I was eventually discharged and I returned to complete my studies. I was successful that year with an eighty-five per cent grade. I took the academic notes from my friends and I read them, not wanting to waste a moment except occasionally when with Borka who would go with me to the banks of river Danube, just to refocus on my lives' hope and aspirations, and sometimes for a good, deserving and satisfying cuddle. My heart now was actively giving me joy as it works efficiently well—but what led to the initial state of helplessness might be due to my inability in the past to access modern medical facilities. Would I be able to say that the Nigeria in which I grew up with all the import earnings of cotton, skin and hide, tin, cocoa, coal, timber, petroleum and other mineral resources could not afford to equip her health facilities? How many souls who did not have the benefit of being in Europe would have been long buried and perhaps forgotten in their thousands? This might not be unconnected with the system that has created such a dent into our national psyche and made for us a new tribe of mourners. Thank God after many years of continual medical care and rigorous tests, I became healthy, and this robust health was what I never had since I was a child. The strength in me now having overcome my heart and palpitation problems is so amazing. From my fiftieth birthday I enjoy a new lease of life to the full, riding bicycles and walking up to twelve kilometres in a stretch.

Slovenia, the Land of the Gospel

As one who originally trained to be an Engineer, I discovered on my return to Slovenia that the caring, loving God was indeed being worshipped in Yugoslavia and also discovered a ministry into a priestly vocation, both of which shaped the rest of my life. Even when I felt emotionally tortured by some events of the past, I got the grace which enabled me hold on to my vision of God. In June 1988, I was at a prayer meeting in Ljubljana, Slovenia when it was announced that a revival service would be held somewhere up country in Slovenia as part of the youth programme. I volunteered to be there, and no persuasions could deter me from joining although I was more than the age limit for being a youth. In Yugoslavia as in the majority of Europe, you could not be thirty years old and still claim to be a youth, and the ages of between 15-20 years old would be the expected. This is not so where I came from. A youth may be defined as anyone still around forty-five years, and many of the ones who remained members of the youth clubs, in the community or Church like Young Men Christian Association or Young Women Christian Association or The Youth League could be in their seventies or eighties. To many people youthfulness is the individual's concept of being young. I told them you are as old or young as you feel; besides we are all children of our parents and of God. The word children were used more symbolically as a pun here rather than being a biological baby of a parent. It was at that youth conference that I listened to the sermon that changed my life. The atmosphere was lively because there was much to eat and drink, and in fact the expected entertainment was part of the attraction that lured me to the event to escape the boredom of staying at home during the bank holidays during which time the conference was to last. However, the speaker was not the normal type of evangelist that I was expecting to see, as the man was dragging his speech, slow and not charismatic, without the usual attendant mannerism of many evangelists. I therefore was going out intermittently more to take a piece of cake, drink a cup of tea, or go for a bite of turkey or meat than sitting in the hall and listening to him. He was preaching in Dutch language but his sermon was being interpreted at the same time in English and Slovene languages which gave me a double opportunity of hearing him. At one point I refused to leave the hall despite all the encouragements of Buki for a short walk outside, as something the man was saying seemed to be relevant and worthy of listening to. At the point when he gave the altar call, I was one of the first set of people to get to the front of the church, not quite knowing what to expect but recognising that I was indeed a sinner searching for repentance, with a willingness to surrender my life to Jesus. The old and boring preacher did manage to convince me that there is a God, and that Jesus Christ is the Redeemer of the world. Before this event I had felt disappointment in the collaborative role of Christian leaders in the abuse that happened in Africa. I can remember how I had in the past unashamedly stormed out of a church, muttering about all the idiotic banging on about Jesus as they held up their hands in adoration to Jesus in worship. To be honest, at that time, the mere mention of the name of Jesus made me feel embarrassed, and worshipping Jesus as Lord seemed to me ridiculous. I felt God's love on me that afternoon as the evangelist prayed for me and I opened my eyes to a whole new world. I started seeing people from this time in a completely different way, understanding them in a way that I have never done before. Living and loving gradually became real and very meaningful for me and I saw that the world in which I live is not entirely the same as the 19th century Africa, and the Europeans of today were not the colonialists of previous generations. They moved on from that position a long time back. I realised I was surrounded by friends who encouraged me and supported me as I moved forward with the art of living. It was at this time that I realised that if not for Jesus, I would never have come into this world. Just then and during this revival programme, I reaffirmed my love to Jesus as my Lord and Saviour. Two months after this event I was to transfer my studies from Ljubljana in Slovenia to continue my post graduate degree programme at the University of Vienna, Austria. During the familiarisation trip to Vienna to meet with my new supervisor and see the facilities, God met with me in a special way as the Provider and the Almighty One. The journey from the beginning to my return to Slovenia remained for me a miracle as God met Buki and I with his provisions and directions in an amazing way. We returned to Ljubljana to pack our things and complete the required paper work for our transfer, but this was not to be. God definitely had other plans and He made this explicit to me twice within twenty four hours in a dream and the events that unfolded. I called Mihail Kuzmic, our pastor in Ljubljana to book an appointment, but on picking up the phone he invited us to lunch because he too wanted to have a word with me about something bothering him. As we entered his house, and before I could explain why I needed to see him, he simply gave me an address with the telephone number of the Evangel Theology Faculty in Osijek, Croatia and requested me to consider it. I was confounded, because up until then my wife had not agreed to my thinking of a career change, as she insisted, "I married an engineer, not a pastor". We ate our lunch quietly and as fast as we could, we departed the pastor's house. I decided I had to see the seminary and perhaps talk with Faculty about the prerequisites, and the admission process. In all these, my wife would not budge. Suddenly, after sitting silently for what appeared to be a long time, she asked me if she could say something and that would decide her final vote. I encouraged her to ask any question as we tried our possible best to look for the answers. She then said "if it would be possible for the seminary authorities to meet us at the train station, then she would agree God had wanted us to go to Osijek". This was quite a shock to me, and I told her this would be absolutely impossible. We were already on the train to Osijek and it was not the time of mobile phones. It was quite impossible to contact the school or ask them to meet us, besides we had neither spoken a word to anyone there, nor even obtained the admission forms, what test would this be? When she would not change her mind, I was preparing myself for the worst as I was evaluating the implication of going solo into ministry if she would not cooperate. However, to our greatest surprise, by the time we arrived at the rail station at Osijek, we found Damir, the college secretary was waiting for us. There was an announcement from the station Public Address System asking us to meet Damir at the 'meeting point'. My wife and I were shocked to the marrow. How did the college know we were on our way? I was later told that the pastor at Ljubljana called my house to ask about my welfare, only for him to understand through a friend that we were on our way down to the institution in Osijek. He must have felt so happy or relieved to realise we were making the trip, and he called the school to assist us with orientation. God works in miraculous ways, and God could lead others to assist us! God saved both my marriage and ministry with that action. At the Evangel Theology Faculty in Osijek, Croatia I had the incredibly huge blessing to be guided by the Bob and Sheryl Beard, missionaries from the United States of America and by Peter Kuzmic, the dean of the Faculty and Miroslav Volf, a visiting professor from Germany taught me New Testament studies. On graduation in 1991, we returned to Ljubljana and started working to raise funds for our trip back to Nigeria, but God knew when we had enough, and so an innocent letter about the health of our first son who was recovering from malaria in Nigeria made us move back in haste to Nigeria.

God continually watching over us

The story of the sovereign God watching over the world and especially those who look up to him for support and trusting him and obedient to him has been with me since my elementary school days. How I got this story I cannot remember, but as a child playing or before saying our evening prayers I used to look out to see if God was still there in Heaven, and he was, and He is still there. The assurances of God remaining true came out strongly in my years in Slovenia, and England when I needed assurance that I was not alone through some difficult periods of my life. I would look out for the moon, and always find the picture of the King as he seems to be always there showering his blessings upon me, after I had said my simple prayer' *God, I am your son, I am still here and I know you are looking at me and praying for me.*' I shall then say other prayers, and through my life in Africa, America, Middle-East and in Europe, the picture of the King of Kings has not changed, his constant position of blessing me is always there, and I had not been disappointed in the God my Father and his Son, Jesus Christ in whom I believe. My father had also always pointed out to me that God is bigger than his image in the moon, because not even the moon can accommodate him, but the picture of him is to continually remind us that He is always God present with us.

Chapter Three

In the Church Of Nigeria

Ijebu Diocese

When Henry Townsend and others arrived Badagry in about 1842, where they built the first storey building, the Yoruba of the south-west Nigeria accepted the Gospel. This led to the arrival of ex-slaves like Samuel Ajayi Crowther being returned to Abeokuta and the Lagos area by the missionaries and merchants but they were restricted to the Lagos colony because the Ijebu which incidentally is my sub-group, did not allow the railway any access through their land. They neither allowed Ijebu ex-slaves to return home nor allowed ex-slaves any passage through Ijebuland. In fact the Ijebu did not trust the Europeans because they feared that this might be a precursor to another slavery expedition. This led to the Imagbon war of 1892, when the British used their canons and other superior fire-arms to subdue the Ijebu. It was after this war that christianity got into Ijebuland long after some other parts of Yorubaland of the southwest Nigeria had received the Christian gospel. Once the Ijebu were conquered, they accepted Christianity and became part of the evangelistic programme. According to Wikipedia, Henry Townsend (1815-1886) was an Anglican missionary in Nigeria. Ordained in England in 1842, Townsend set off for Sierra Leone, landing there that same year. After working there only a few months, he was transferred to the Yoruba mission. From 1846 to 1867, he based his mission in Abeokuta with Samuel Ajayi Crowther who became the first indigenous Anglican Bishop. He retired in 1876. According to Ward 2011, Ijebu, unlike most of the Yoruba city states, had remained adamantly closed to Christian missionaries (British and Yoruba) until the British expedition in 1892. Nevertheless, many Ijebu (including Holy Johnson) had migrated to Lagos where they became influenced by Christianity. After the catastrophe of defeat and once the ruler had accepted missionaries, Christianity made great strides in Ijebu—it had the highest growth rates in Nigeria over the following twenty years or so, and became a leading part of the Anglican church in Nigeria. Islam equally made striking gains during this time. Ijebu Diocese was carved out from Lagos Diocese and inaugurated as a diocese on the 8th August 1976. Bishop Abraham Oluwole Olowoyo became the second diocesan Bishop after Bishop Omowaiye Akintemi who was the pioneer Bishop. Bishop Oluwole set up many of the structures and ethics that guided the Diocese during my time in Ijebu diocese. He was a great teacher and preacher. According to Ijebu Diocese (2010), 'Christianity was not embraced in Erunwon-Ijebu before 1893 due to the powerful influence of the pagan Oba Agbeluwo, the Elerunwon of Erunwon and his Osugbo Council as nobody dared profess the Christian religion. However in 1894, the Christians in Erunwon braced up and sent a delegation to the Oba to formally request for a piece of land to build a Church. Miraculously, the Oba consented and demanded forty pounds as compensation for the land. The second delegation secured the land on the payment of forty pounds and 24 small bottles of Schnapps'. This traditionalist Oba Agbeluwo from Ipatun quarter of Erunwon was my progenitor and the pagan rituals of the time demands that his son—Adegbasaiye, should be interred along with his father once the King passed into the hereafter. Fortunately for my grandfather whose mother was loved and respected by the Odi in the palace she was warned. The Ogbeni Odi who was the head of the Palace guards and servants informed her to run with the baby boy and she ran to her father at Oja-Omo, who incidentally was the Magusen of Itamarun. The Magusen could not allow his grandson, a prince of another realm to live in his palace; hence he procured a land where he settled him along with some people to live with him at Okepo, Ijebu Imusin. Hence Prince Adegbasaiye now known as John Adenaiya Adesanya with a set of new names was not known to relatives and people of Erunwon but lived close to his mother's family in Ijebu Imusin. Prince John Adenaiya Adesanya grew up a Christian and with a few others started St. Mary's Anglican (CMS) Church when the authorities introduced new guidelines to the worshippers at St Mary's (Roman Catholic) Church also in Ijebu Imusin. They were insisting that polygamists could no longer take Holy Communion in Church, and that the extra women surplus to the first wife must be sent away. My grandfather and some few others started the Church and invited the Church Missionary Society (CMS) to take it over. Both the Anglican and the Roman Catholic Churches in my home town became thriving churches, and my home church is the seat of the Ijebu-Imusin Archdeaconry. When I was growing up, St. Mary's Church seemed to me the biggest church in the world but I have since realised that was wishful thinking. My call into the ministry came quite early in life but was deliberately ignored, and at some points denied. I recollect when I was in the third year of my secondary education and at the age of 15, one of my father's close friends started referring to me as a Reverend gentleman, and when I got to class four, for whatever reason, he started to address me as a Reverend canon. This particular man addressed me as a Venerable Archdeacon for most of my last year in the secondary school until I started writing my GCE O/L when he started addressing me as Bishop. This to me was an irritation as I hated to be associated with the church or the personalities of a priest. I could not see in me anything churchy, to be so insulted or ridiculed from my father's friend. This unsung prophet whose name is Odutayo, was formerly a police officer who later became a School teacher, hence he was known as 'Olopa School' meaning the 'School police'. He was a man with wonderful communication skills. I was one of the clergy who, receiving a vocation at an early age resisted the call, but instead set for myself some other lofty goals believing to know what was better. At the time of my youth, I preferred to be a Lawyer or a Doctor, but never a priest. I wanted to be a great and important person in life, but what actually described greatness and importance in life became a life-long debate. In the early 1970s, the fire of the liberation movements was consuming the hearts of the youth in Africa, and liberation theology was gaining much ground. At that time, the fight against apartheid was on-going and the issues of black emancipation and liberation slogans were indeed a more attractive discussion for my friendship cohort than talk about christianity. More so, the ministry was without any attraction to me then, as the models of society were lawyers, doctors or engineers, and I was focused on either becoming a doctor or an engineer, but I had a natural interest in the arts. How God prepared me for ministry remains an interesting part of my life. After I had finished secondary school and passed my GCE examinations, I went on to sit as a private GCE A/L candidate in Economics, English literature and Bible knowledge. This was within seven months of leaving secondary school at the completion of my GCE O/L because I felt one of my friends challenged my intellect. Without any further education and with the help of self-tutorial books, I managed to pass Economics and Literature which was quite a massive surprise to me as I did not have the privilege of attending any class in Economics while in school as I went to a grammar school, where such subjects were not taught. I was offered admission to study Yoruba language at the University of Lagos and Printing Technology at Yaba College of Technology, Lagos. The London School of Printing, Elephant and Castle, London; and The Sheffield Polytechnic, UK also offered me a place to study but all the overseas admissions lapsed as I could not afford the cost. Two years later, I received the Federal Government of Nigeria scholarship to study in Serbia, then one of the constituent states of the Socialist Federal Republic of Yugoslavia. On my return to Nigeria, after graduating from the Evangel Theology Faculty, I was made a Deacon in June 1991 at Epiphany Anglican Church, Eruwon-Ijebu at the Trinity Ordination. One other person—Rev Otenaike, was preparing to be made deacon in Ekiti Diocese the following year who is a direct descendant of one of those who went to Oba Agbeluwo to negotiate the land on which to build a Church at Erunwon. I was deaconed, a direct descendant of the pagan Oba who released the land on which stands the Church where I was made a Deacon. I took a deep breath immediately after Bishop Oluwole has finished the service and with a profound sense of history, I smiled. There I was a new Deacon at Erunwon, a young man who would perhaps never have been born. Though my grandfather was forced into exile and poverty due to pagan practices, I returned as a beneficiary of my progenitor's agreement to give the piece of land to the young Christian Church. My priesthood Ordination Service at The Cathedral Church of Our Saviour, Italowajoda, Ijebu-Ode attracted another kind of personalities. Since the building of the Church and before the inauguration of Ijebu Diocese, the name used to be St. Saviour's Church, a Church which was an elegant spectacle to behold as it seemed to stand on a little hill and you can enter the Church through some steps from Folagbade Road. Folagbade Road, used to be the centre of commerce in the town and what you didn't get to buy on Folagbade Road could only be found either in Lagos or London. My father sold leather boxes, Umbrellas, Sandals and Shoes on 95 Folagbade Road and popularly known as 'Kilodu' which is the Ijebu version for Claudius. Beside Kilodu's Shoe shop was the patient medicine Store for Courage. Courage was a nickname and not his original name, but I was not aware of his correct names. Courage was a popular figure and his family house was just across the road. Just to the right and beside Courage's shop was the Glass Shop owned by Mr. Okeowo. Mr Okeowo's wife was a School teacher and they were not only more educated than most people, they were wealthy, and beside this Glass Shop was Eto Brothers, Plumbing Services. Across the road from the Glass Shop was the Shoe Shop of my father's gentle friend. He was more than his friend; he was a soul mate and brother. His name was Yaya Disu. He was a gentleman and never seen to be angry. You have to listen properly to hear the man speak. He was the epitome of simplicity, a great man. But he was well known as Baba Ramo, because his first child is named Ramota. My father had other great friends like Johnson Sangode with whom he shared childhood adventures, Otulana, and Odutayo. Folagbade Road was the centre of trade to most Ijebu when I was growing up, and yes, my father was one of the major players. Some years ago, the newly created Ogun State Government turned Folagbade Road into a double carriage way, and this act affected the business capacity of Folagbade Road and also in the process removed some of the stairs leading into Our Saviour's Cathedral Church. Today instead of the ancient beautiful steps, a wall covered with ceramics partitioned the lower side of the building from the road view. I hope that the new Cathedral Church Building may be able to restore some of the lost glory. I finished primary education in December 1968 and had a gap year in 1969 before starting secondary School in January 1970. During my gap year I lived briefly with my senior brother-Ademolu who was a student of Ijebu Ode Grammar School, also lives in the Shoe Shop. The Shop was partitioned into two. The front side with shelves full of shoes and sandals with other items, and the back was for a small sized bed for my brother and the shop floor where I would lie on the mat at night. Though the space was tight yet it was glorious living in Ijebu-Ode in those days. One Sunday morning, instead of going to Church, I went with my brother Idowu who was also visiting to assist one of our sisters who at that time was a personal Helper to Mrs Okeowo do the house chores, washing clothes, cleaning and sweeping. We would have finished the entire task before Mr & Mrs Okeowo return from the Church service. This was not because we were kind-hearted or charitable, but because it was an opportunity to share with our senior sister her delicious Sunday morning breakfast consisting of sliced-bread, margarine and the ever alluring cup of tea with milk. Our sister would ensure that all work was done before paying us with a share of her food. One morning, on our way to the Shoe Shop after assisting our sister, we were admiring the shining black colour of a Mercedes Benz car, in front of St. Saviour's Church, Italowajoda, cherishing our reflection on the well-polished car, when suddenly some people pounced upon us and they beat us into a state of stupor. The crowd of people pleading for our lives gathered around the car, and at a point, the service at St. Saviour's Church must have stopped. The owner of the car along with some notable people of the town and the Priest came out to examine us. They marched through the church doors down the steps, and one of the chiefs sarcastically asked why we touched the car? Neither my brother nor myself was in any position to speak, as people realised that my senior brother had fainted. The owner of the car, probably the most powerful man in Ijebu-Ode at a point, a former politician and high ranking chief could not be bothered, as he turned back into the Church without uttering a word and the priest and others followed him to continue the Church service. My brother was in hospital for close to ten days before he was discharged. At my Priesthood ordination, some of the Muslims who were friends of my father and witnessed that gory 1969 incident were present at my Ordination at the Cathedral Church of Our Saviour, but they were not confounded until I was posted as Cathedral Priest in 1995.

It was history made when I preached at the Cathedral benefitting from the generosity of the owner of the 1969 car incident for the first time. It was Christ at work when I was called upon to minister to the man, standing in for his priest who was unavoidably absent for a Home Communion for him in 1992. On that day after the service, I became friends with this man. That is the power of Christ Jesus at work. I am happy to say that my father's gentle friend became a Christian with most of his house-hold before he died.

ii. Archbishop Vining College of Theology, Akure

I was still struggling to come to terms with what has happened to Bishop Olowoyo when I was told to prepare for a move to Archbishop Vining College of Theology, Akure as a lecturer of pastoral psychology, care and counselling, but on arrival and within a month of my appointment, I was made the acting Registrar of the college. I was saddled partly with the responsibility of effecting the successful take off of the college degree programme with the University of Ibadan, with whom the college was being affiliated. At Archbishop Vining College of Theology (AVCTA), I over-saw the training of those preparing for Christian ministry and I must confess that I am blessed being part of that team. It is a great privilege to train people for ministry; although I had concerns for the approach of most Nigerian bishops to the staffing of the seminaries. I was able to be closely involved, and pleased to see some able and competent people go through clergy training with many of them becoming senior priests and bishops in the Nigerian church. It was while I was at A.V.C.T, Akure that in 1999 I was made Canon of the Cathedral of Our Saviour in Ijebu diocese and appointed in 2003, the Archdeacon of Iwade Archdeaconry, and vicar of Emmanuel church, Italupe, Ijebu Ode. In 2003 I was installed by Bishop Omoyajowo, as the Archdeacon of Iwade archdeaconry that covered an area that was later divided into seven archdeaconries within the diocese. The vicarage, the church plus the hall were within the downtown of Ijebu Ode which is populated by Christians, Muslims and traditionalists.

Sometimes, fetish priests and priestesses would dance past our compound for their rituals, while the female folks of whatever religion were forbidden to see the Agemo masquerade. Even though many of the leaders of these cults live in modern day houses and some were in the higher rungs of educational and socio-economic ladder of the society. Strangely too, those who are in traditional religions would still prefer to be known as Muslims in the mosques on Fridays and as Christians in the churches on Sundays. My study of counselling psychology together with my study in theology obviously helped my ministry in all the places where I had been privileged to serve. As a priest, I discovered quite early that counselling and spirituality have a lot to gain from each other and of course they complement each other. I am happy for the Church of England with their ministerial provisions; it is a caring Church and is very concerned about the welfare and continuous ministerial clergy development. Bishop John for example is noted for asking about the priests and other Church officers, he sends e-mails, visits, and makes phone calls to know how the clergy are faring in their personal lives and ministry. Some other Provinces may not want to be bothered. I have been left traumatised by the suspicions of the leadership with whom I have served at AVCT, Akure who feared for their position because I have a doctorate degree. I was the first serving Lecturer to have a doctorate degree at Archbishop Vining College of Theology, Akure. There is an assumption that you need such degrees to head a degree awarding institution, but in Nigeria of my time, other mundane considerations were stronger qualifications. I had arrived AVCT, Akure and later enrolled for my Ph. D degree programme at The Ondo State University which later changed to The University of Ado-Ekiti. I was of course posted to AVCT, Akure because some felt that I was academically inclined and that the Seminary posting was beneficial. The 'old-students' link in Nigeria is very strong. There is a loss to anyone in Nigeria who do not have strong collegial connections. I did not attend any of the Theology Schools in Nigeria. Some felt that my doctorate study was a scheme to become the Dean at Archbishop Vining College of Theology, Akure where I was a lecturer. They could not see any justification for obtaining a Doctor of Philosophy degree and therefore imputed ideas. I have reasons to believe there were discriminatory considerations. In spite of my personal challenges at that time, which could not be handled in Nigeria and for which I returned to Europe, some opined that I was only 'stooping to conquer'. I knew of priests in similar situations in the past who died in post and I was determined to avert this. Therefore I took steps to seek the understanding and cooperation of my diocesan bishop, Bp. E. Ayodele Awosoga, from whom I obtained the necessary permission and clearance.

The Emmanuel Church, Italupe

By 2003, before I was appointed as an Archdeacon, I had already penned three books and one of them 'The Sexes under God' is visible in many parishes. One day I travelled to Ilorin, Kwara state of Nigeria which is in the middle belt, and for the two days that I was away, I was privileged to meet three people who had seen my book and had read it. I was being invited to lead Bible studies, give lectures and address gatherings, on the one topic on which I have written extensively and on which my masters and doctorate degrees are based,—the issue of marriage, sex and family. As a clergyman by virtue of my counselling and vocation, I had suddenly been transformed from being the shy person that I was from my youth to one who could look the opposite sex in the face and tell her how she could have her man for keeps using the gifts, God had given her. It is a transformation from a shy, quiet, introvert and easily intimidated person into a public-speaking figure. It was apparent that my time as Archdeacon of Iwade and Vicar of Emmanuel Church, Italupe, which coincidentally was the time I served as the Synod secretary of Ijebu Diocese, was a very busy time. I developed a habit of hard work and my commitment to counselling education, coupled with my Social concern involvements in and out of the Diocese kept me going. The service of installation and collation as Archdeacon at Emmanuel Church, Italupe was a celebrated joy. Through the service and throughout the day and the night before, I was feeling the gravity of the responsibility before me. That is the oldest place in Ijebuland where the Christian gospel was first preached. Emmanuel Church to which

I had been posted is a big church and perhaps one of the largest churches in Ijebu-land, with quite a bit of historicity, a great Church with very long traditions of doing things cast in marble and which had in her unbroken cherished history always had spiritual giants from different backgrounds as their vicars and archdeacons. At the creation of Ijebu diocese, the vicarage at Italupe served as the Bishop's court, while their administrative office served as the Diocesan office, such was the reputation and influence of the Church within the scheme of things in Ijebu diocese, hence my anxiety and hope to thrive in such an environment. In this environment, I saw myself as an underdog being appointed from among a cream of clergy who have experience and with some having more Church exposure than myself. This is a congregation that averaged five hundred and fifty every Sunday and the administration within the archdeaconry, of a staff of about 18 among which were senior priests, demanded strenuous hours of patient administration and meditation, and sometimes some anxious moments which were a big strain on my health and family peace. Many years ago, I could not comprehend believing a clergyman if I have been told by a clergyman how busy he was. Stress was taking its toll on me as I spent up to fifteen hours in the office during my early days at Italupe as I went through all the files in a systematic manner ensuring that I briefed myself since it was the death of my predecessor in office that was the catalyst that brought me to the post and I was not privileged to receive any hand-over note as to the situation of things in either the Church or the Archdeaconry. However, with a bit of hindsight, it became for me a benefit that I was able to get my information from the minutes of Diocesan, Archdeaconry and PCC files before listening to witnesses whose testimonials were sometimes coloured or biased according to their own perspectives, and because some thought of abusing my newness with tainted information. The stress of my workload therefore became for me a catalyst that propelled my mission and vision to see that Italupe Church continues to grow but above all, a Church nurtured by the word of God. A Church that is active in mission to the neighbourhood, witnessing Christ Jesus by way of Social Concern. As in many church organisations, the life of the clergy can be a lonely one, apart for prayer and meditations, I had to set myself apart from things that might entangle me and distract my ministry. Yet I must adequately be present and represent the people if I am to continue representing them before God on the Altar of Grace in worship. I therefore saw to it that all my assistant clergy and vicars were enabled to perform their roles effectively. I stuck to the federal nature of governance allowing every committee, evangelist, clergy the space and pace to be what they are appointed or paid to do, with my task being supervisory in nature and doing those things which I must perform as my statutory responsibility. This helped reduce the overwhelming burden of administration. Leaving the Church of Nigeria was not an easy decision to make for me, as it was therefore with huge pains that I left Nigeria once again and also for the fact that I was enjoying a thriving ministry at Italupe. The congregation was very responsive and things were happening in the Church, the Archdeaconry and in the Diocese. It was exciting combining my numerous roles, being a vicar, archdeacon, synod secretary and secretaries to the statutory committees of the Diocesan Board and Finance Board. Emmanuel Church was developing in leaps and bounds with a flourishing budget. What with a new hostel just built for students use at the University of Education on Ijagun Road, a house just donated to the Church by a well-wisher and about to be refurbished, the re-roofing of Emmanuel parish Church with long span aluminium sheets just completed, the purchase of a giant generator to serve the church community, and a fleet of buses and an official car—all these made possible by the generous donations of people of goodwill and a supportive parish council within three years. There was an average Sunday attendance of about 615 people consisting of the Children's Sunday school, 7am Holy communion service in Yoruba language, 8am Morning Prayer in English language, 10am Corporate worship which is the main service and the 6pm Youth fellowship in English language. This was beside the mid-week services of Bible study, women's fellowship and the Boys and Girls brigade and the choir practice. The 10am main service would normally last from 10am till sometimes about 1pm, but on other special days, it was not abnormal to be in the church still praying and worshipping God a little bit more time, with all smiles and happiness, most especially during the first Sunday of the month because of the Eucharist. These were possible also because of the co-operation from the congregation. There was room for me since my installation and induction to assume a Pentecostal type of leadership in the Church. The Spirit of God used the circumstance of my appointment to enable me act more actively and decisively without the PCC creating any hindrance. At any point when I had a vision in the Church, I would go ahead with it praying and soliciting the PCC to buy into it and they normally approve. Barely two months into my arrival at Italupe, I unsettled the hornet's horn, after a period of rain I noticed some leakages from the roof. I felt depressed. The Spirit of the prophet in me was aroused, but I hate a leaking roof. I declared during the service that the roof must be changed at once. The roof problem had been a sore issue in Italupe for many years and the wise and elderly thought I should just keep quiet about it to maintain the peace. This irritated me the more as I was for the roof to be changed, I could not even settle for a repair but a complete change of roofing. In the course of that month I was aroused during a service to start a Fund-raising for the new roof I was proposing and for two months, I went on, and God blessed the effort that brought in about one-third of the needed funds even before I mentioned it to the PCC, and the Church treasurer kept noticing that money was coming into Church coffers. I do not handle money personally in my ministry and I do not help Churches to make purchases, the treasurer is always the spending officer. Eventually, the roof was changed from asbestos roofing sheets into long-span Aluminium roofing sheets. It became a main attraction, more so without any more leakages. For the success of this project the Church Building committee which consisted of hard working and committed members worked day and night, chaired by Engr. Babafemi Osoba and his deputy Pa A. Daodu. After this and barely having a respite, I started raising funds for the re-painting of the Church. At this time the congregation had bought-in into my leadership and style. They supported the project fully, and when the funds for the repainting of all the buildings were ready, I negotiated the donation of a Library within the premises from Niyi Osibogun, and he also equipped the Library. Then the paintings were done. It was a pretty transformation for the Church premises. At this time I was beginning to contemplate the restoration of the Church Hall, when the Spirit of God led me to think of having investments for the

Church. I negotiated two things with Christianah Alagbalawura, a donation of a piece of two plots of land, on Ijagun road, Ijebu Ode and we built a Students" Hostel, with many of the materials used being donated, and Christianah later gave the Church a car which served as the first official car for the Vicar of Italupe. I invited a Broker to give us a talk on the Stock market, and we purchased some more shares in reputable companies adding to what the Church originally had. Then I agreed with the PCC to refurbish a building of four flats that the Church had on Igbeba Road, and a complete renovation took place. Just as we have just bought another Commuter Bus to augment what we originally owned to help bring people to Church, we got a donation of a house on Imoru road, Ijebu Ode, from Mama Itunu Oyemade. She made this bequest to Italupe and the building was renovated for tenants to move in. Within my forty months tenure at Italupe, we discarded the age-old generator that was not able to adequately serve the premises, and we raised Funds to buy a new high powered Generator. I raised about one-third of the total cost in a spur of the moment, the day I first raised the issue in Church. It was purchased and installed and our electric power problem was solved. During this time, we printed evangelistic Tracts for our outreach programmes, intensified weekly Bible study and mission to the immediate communities of the Church, which was home to the muslims and the traditionalists. The Spirit of God also made it possible for us to strengthen the Social concern ministry to the needy and the sick, giving as much assistance for school fees and help with apprenticeship of the children of the neighbourhood. The Osibogun family came in with help in the scholarships grants in the memory of their mother. When it became clear to us that our first Bus was not delivering in terms of quality and service, we sold the big Nissan Bus and replaced it with a smaller, but more serviceable one. By the time I was leaving Italupe in November 2006, we bought another Bus to help fully with transporting people to the Church and from their homes. Money was not a problem, as everything our hearts desire, God provided. God gave us vision, funds and willing hearts. The Church of Christ experienced a glorious time, but my health was failing fast, and I needed to do something about it quickly. All this time because of the anxiety my health has caused my loved ones in the past, I have learnt how to keep my own counsel regarding my health, therefore it was not such a surprise that some were unsympathetic as I travelled up and down Europe, as they thought I must be very rich to afford such a luxury. In 2005 Bishop Ayodele first muted the idea that it would be better for me to relocate back to Europe, but by 2006 it was obvious that would be the reasonable thing to do. Instead of leaving for Europe, I returned to Archbishop Vining College of Theology, Akure, to resume teaching, because I thought I was tired of living abroad, but within three months of my return to Akure, my health relapsed seriously, and it was glaring that I should return to Europe. While I was at Italupe, I oversaw the renewal of Emmanuel Church, which transformed the Church complex and created new buildings and public spaces and improved the facilities of its ministry to the people. This turned me into a Fund-raiser, as I saw that the money could be used for good and as part of the engine room for the way the Christian Gospel is conveyed. I tried never to forget that the Church exists for the community, most especially those who were in dire need or distress. Yes, with a supportive Parochial Church Council, there is no limit to what good a Church can achieve.

Chapter Four

The Social Concern

From 1991 till 2006, I served in different capacities in the Church of Nigeria, first as Team Vicar at St. Paul's Church, Igbaga, Ijebu-Imusin. Apart from my role as Chaplain to the Bishop from 1992-1994, I was also pioneer Prison and Hospital Chaplain in Ijebu diocese from 1992-1998; and pioneer minister coordinating issues of Social concern, with organising practical help to our communities from 1993-1998. I had the privilege of starting the Prison and Hospital chaplaincy in Ijebu Ode in reaction to the death of one of my cousins who died unattended after a road accident. This cousin of mine in company of a friend had gone on a motor bike to visit another friend at Ijebu-Igbo, and to celebrate a Muslim festival marking the end of Ramadan fasting. On their return they had an accident. My cousin fatally injured and was taken to the hospital by another good Samaritan. His unconscious friend recovered to notice on the stretcher lying beside him my cousin who at that time was gasping for breath. In confusion this friend walked out of the hospital into no particular direction, he was found some days later. The doctor on duty gave a prescription and the nurses simply dropped it on my cousin who was on a stretcher in the hospital corridor, as the hospital had no drugs while the victim's family were not aware of his dilemma. I was then a deacon in the village where coincidentally my cousin was head teacher of the village school. The news filtered into the village of his death and it was a time of mourning for both the school and the church along with our family and friends. Later after my priesthood ordination, and juggling between my job as the Chaplain to the Bishop and the needy, it dawned on me to set up the Prison and Hospital Chaplaincy. I circulated a letter to those whom I knew could out of goodwill assist the less-privileged in the society requesting for funds and materials such as clothing, guaranteed grants to pay for the apprenticeship and equipping of both the prison tailoring and carpentry departments. A sum of money was raised from well-meaning individuals and some funds were deposited with the hospital management while a savings account in the name of Ijebu Diocese hospital and prison chaplaincy Fund was opened and the Account passbook kept with the Administrative assistant to the bishop of Ijebu diocese. My visit to the prison as the Bishop's chaplain in company of the diocesan board in 1992 during the celebration of the 100 years of Christianity in Ijebuland and 150 years of Christianity in Nigeria led to the start of a full-fledged diocesan committee for Social Concern. Many volunteers from across the diocese came to the rescue and a full time social concern worker was employed. The ultimate vision was to see that prisoners on discharge were rehabilitated into the community, with training and work enhancement, and that no one should die in our hospitals just for the mere financial reasons of not being able to procure medication. The Diocesan See of Ijebu Ode is situated beside the Benin-Lagos expressway through which travellers going out of Lagos towards the east, and some northern parts of Nigeria would traditionally ply and therefore the hospital there was a reference point whenever there was any major accident, receiving a lot of travelling casualties whose fate might be sealed for lack of funds for medicaments. This committee for which I was privileged to serve as co-ordinator also enabled many people to learn trades and have their school fees paid, without which many would have become school drop-outs. We were of the opinion that helping one member of a family to be self-sufficient would rub off effectively on his or her family and the society would be able to have some more peace. We were concerned for the well-being of the have-nots, and the presence of things that could boost the self-esteem and the confidence of the generality of the people, therefore we were always delighted when some of the ex-convicts were able to pass their GCEs and one or two went on to the University and eventually graduated. We were happy to see a man whose family had lost any hope for his or her survival walk out of the hospital, a healthier person with the assistance and help that Ijebu Diocesan Committee for Social Concern could render. We were happy to assist an aged and poor woman rebuild part of her damaged room, the wall of which fell overnight. She was in danger of greater harm and insecurity if we had not allowed God to use us for His purpose to rebuild her shelter. It was sad that we also had our own share of the societal woes as on one occasion one of the ex-convicts whom we had assisted to get a job and further assisted to become more integrated into the community led a gang of armed robbers who attacked the Bishop's court and in the process inflicted serious injury on our Bishop. I thank God that Bishop Olowoyo did not take it personally, for he pushed himself harder to assist our work after this unfortunate event. One sermon he gave after the event spoke about " *the rich not being able to sleep with the two eyes closed as long as the poor were hungry*". This sermon yielded massive fruits for charity. On another occasion we found that some folks tried to abuse the generosity of the Diocese by trying to make fraudulent financial claims while presenting us with dubious pictures of their socio-economic predicament. At another incident, armed robbers invaded the Diocesan Office and the Bishop Chaplain's residence where I live with my family. The robbers have removed a window from the house when my wife woke me. I was unhappy because I enjoyed my sleep, but she said it appeared we have guests in the house. I took my walking stick, not because of any disability, for it is fashionable for Nigerian men to use walking sticks. I got to the window just in time to see someone climbing into the house through the space where the window used to be. I gave a big shout at the man asking what he thought he was doing and a bang with my bamboo walking stick. He fell back on the ground, and for about an hour his mates were attending to him on the Office space. We had night guards, but the guards did not resurface until the daybreak and when the robbers had gone. Psalm 127.1 says '*Unless the LORD watches over a city, the watchmen stand guard in vain*'. On the other hand we noticed that some folks were languishing in want and hunger while the members of their family were in self-denial of the situation to save their ego, so they might not to be seen as incapable of taking good care of their close family members. Sometimes we were in a dilemma of true situations as some people who for example had malaria and needed to procure medicines were also malnourished, for what should be the priority;

food or medicine. We would seek to be guided by the medical staff in the nearby facility that were often referred to as hospitals but has no comparisons to any medical facility in real life. These can best be described as a building shell, sometimes dirty, dusty and unkempt, with little or no medication, the genuineness of the few tablets on the shelf often needed to be ascertained, and because there was no chance of running pipe borne water or electricity, the hygienic situations or ventilation could not be guaranteed. When this is added to the ever present anopheles mosquitoes watching over their next prey, the situation could not be said to be cheerful. According to Ajibola 2011, with Africa's largest population, estimated at 160 million people, Nigeria bears a greater malaria burden than any other country in the world. Over 300,000 Nigerians die each year of the disease. In sub-Sahara Africa, corruption was and may still be present as the mother of all calamities, as it cripples health, education, the transport sectors and government arms while malaria and poverty induced illnesses account for most deaths. Armed robbery, road accidents are also some of the recurring hazards. Often the ill health that were controlled in other countries overseas wiped away hundreds of lives in Africa, such as diabetes, high blood pressure to say the least while scores went blind for lack of basic facilities that were taken for granted in the modern world. Today many struggle to survive, yet lying half-awake for many nights in fear of night marauders who prowled through the night robbing, and may probably rape. The four walls of the prison were full of people who were hopeless before their conviction and full of despair in prison. Without the gospel the prospect of a climb-back to life is very slim. There were more inmates awaiting trials than those actually convicted and the ratio was about 10:1. This was not helped by the way things were at that time, with the corruption that eats deep into the fabric of society and the prevalence of armed robbery and other forms of violence during the day and night. Yet, there was no way in which the young men being daily warehoused into the prison system were being helped to be redeemed by the government agencies as there were no tools and implements at the carpentry and tailoring workshop nor medicament at the prison clinics. The physical and mental rot is better left to imagination. It was sad that such a situation was the lot of a Nigeria in this century with all the petroleum and other wealth of this country. The voluntary agencies such as the Church came to the rescue and with our belief in the redemptive role of God through our Lord Jesus Christ; the Ijebu Anglican Diocese gave as much support as they could possibly give. Sometimes, with donations from churches and individuals, the diocese restored the prison sewing machines into workable conditions and purchased tools that could assist those who wanted to learn those trades. Perhaps, it was good that the Church provided a shoulder—not a broad one, on which others could weep and share their sorrow because the Church herself has other challenges. The Bishop was spurred on by his personal encounter with lack of plenty, and the encounter of the robbery on him to claim that he had paid part of his own due for the societal negligence of the young generation. The kind words and challenging sermons from the Diocesan Bishop motivated those who listened to him at different forums. The Bible study and Sunday services in the prison were intensified and soon we were having a sizable number of people at the prison prayer fellowships, but sometimes people joined us for what they assume were benefits that came to those who came to fellowship meetings. Our sole aim was to be there for those who had been condemned by the world as hopeless and to shine on them this Light that is Christ, with the hope of encouraging them to have another start in life. The Diocese was able to establish a presence within the prison and the hospital, so that people felt they weren't alone anymore, they felt they had someone with them. In the face of poverty and neglect, in the face of many people who were simply walking—dead, hopeless people before coming into prison and still hopeless inside the prison, someone was saying something hopeful to them, and that is—Jesus saves. Bishop Olowoyo was the Bishop who deaconed and priested me but I also imbibed some interests through him which some leaders may not recommend for which I am grateful. He would return from the Provincial Synod or Bishops' meeting and called some of us to share ideas, and sometimes let us know on what issues to pray for in relation to the direction of the Province of Nigeria. He hoped and prayed that the church of Nigeria after their era would be better and he gave encouragement to us to be faithful to Christ for progress, and of course he stopped us in our tracks whenever our speech or actions was seen as reactive.

Bishop Olowoyo died as a result of a fatal motor accident in 1998, and many of us could still not forget how committed, meticulous and courageous he was in the course of the Gospel in Ijebu diocese in his ministry and life. He was the second bishop of the diocese and everyone recognised that Bishop Olowoyo was a strong advocate for socio-economic justice and faithfulness in the church. We were deeply shocked and grieved by the manner of his sudden death, and just like the Biblical Gideon we were tempted to ask, '*what if God was with us*? Indeed God is with us in all these things to support his family and sustain His church. I had earlier served at St Paul's, Igbaga, All Saints Church, Igbeba, Ijebu Ode and also as the Cathedral priest in the Cathedral at Ijebu Ode and I left for Archbishop Vining College, Akure after a brief stay at the Church in Erinlu, Ijebu-Ode.

The Poor Among Us

Many sub-Sahara Africans are suspicious of the western way of life which is seen to be permissive to the extent that everyone does what he or she feels is right. The issue of what is seen as immoral or sinful from the average African point of view might also be suspected as the western celebs lead fashion globally. In many Churches in Africa, it remains unacceptable for a lady to wear trousers, not even a lady's suit with trousers, and ladies are not permitted to be in church without a native dress head gear or hat, any consumption of alcoholic drinks is seen as sinful, neither is it acceptable for ushers and sidemen and ladies in church to dress in native attires. This level of understanding makes many Anglican churches adamant that no woman can minister without a headgear or scarf or hat. The Europeans had fostered some ideas among others with the introduction of Christianity into Africa, and I have taken these three as examples of what came to Africa with the advent of Christianity. First: the Bible talked about men not covering up in church while the woman must not shave her hair and expose her bare head in church. It was a taboo in Jewish culture to have women cut their hair except as an act of punishment and to depict mourning. This also was the tradition of many African societies, but Paul emphasised that the woman's hair remained a covering for her head. Paul teaches that; nature teaches that long hairs meant that women should cover their head (1 Corinthians 11.14). Was putting on a wig therefore a double covering? I guess not, no wonder the Yoruba females normally adorn their heads beautifully with different types of head gears. What justified the opinion of the early missionaries in Africa on this matter might be culturally conditioned also. Perhaps, because they were also of a view on the full import of the Scriptures, or are things changing because even in today's western civilisation, the sight of a lady wearing a hat is rare and probably reserved for the annual Ascot. The Bible does not encourage women to wear men's clothes, yet for many Africans it remained to be seen if the knowledge is clear that there are trousers for males and also for females, because many Africans are yet to know where the difference lies between the two. It is a fact that there are clothes meant for both sexes known as unisex, vests or scarfs and shirts. It may be helpful for the sub-Sahara African Christians to know this and accept the fact that culturally in other lands; people have their own dress styles. Secondly, Alcoholism is subject to cultural definitions. If you ask in Belgrade, 'Does Mr Ivo drinks alcohol'? This will be yes if Mr Ivo is a drunkard, but if he drinks ten bottles of beer without getting drunk, he won't be taken as one who drinks. In Britain, you may find a gentleman drinking a whole bottle of wine after a good dinner. That is not the person you will refer to as using alcohol. It is also usual for some people to use red wine as they prepare delicious meals. This is a cultural thing in Europe and the wine which Nigeria originally produced is Palm wine locally known as 'emu-oguro' or 'burukutu' from wheat. In our traditional way we drink our Palm wine, use it to prepare medicine and for other purposes. In Nigeria, a bottle of wine may be shared between families of four for six days yet they classify themselves as taking alcohol. Everyone tastes alcohol be it in sweets or cakes or other delicacies. The Bible does not encourage either from the Old or New Testament the immoderate use of alcohol or of anything else. Scripture always points us to be moderate in all we do, as excessive acts can lead to perversion. Thirdly, Did it appear to many Africans that Jesus as a man grew in the context of his environment? Therefore it was possible for Jesus who wore the dress of Palestine and ate the food supplied by the people around him to minister to the environment where he lived. Some years ago, my senior brother and I were late for the preliminaries of the choir therefore we did not robe as choristers for that Sunday service. We sat within the congregation. It was the Juvenile Harvest festival of the church and we were in one of our superbly preserved dresses. I was fifteen years old and my brother was about a year older. In proper English, he is my half-brother, being a 'half-brother' is not acceptable word in our family, and it is politically unwise in Nigeria for a Yoruba to address your parents brother or sister or parents age-mates as Uncle or by name, instead they are called Daddy or Mother. My father had two wives and he is the brother through my father's first wife. The service progressed during the singing of the first hymn and the Warden realised that there were not sufficient ushers at the door. Therefore the warden approached my brother and I and enjoined us to man the door. We were honoured to be so consulted but we were initially scared as we had never done this task before, more so as you need a certain level of dress which we could not afford. We were immediately given tutorial as to what we were expected to do at each point, besides there were other ushers in the church to be our guide. Midway into the service, two well-dressed ladies, who incidentally were the children of better educated and wealthy men of the congregation, entered the Church. The warden marched up to my brother and I to relieve us of our responsibilities as Ushers. We were flustered and dazed, as this was a major embarrassment to our parents who along with the congregation watched the scenario and our shame. We felt disgraced. We were crest fallen as we left the door, and instead of finding another seat on the pews we walked out from the usher's seat to find a place for ourselves at the back of the Church. We had always worn our school uniform to join the choir, but on this festival service, we had worn our Sunday best, the Christmas dress we put on for the second time ever during the year for this Juvenile Harvest festival. I had no shoes on but my esteemed rubber sandals, and it was not enough to be an usher in our local church. The humiliation felt from merely looking at our friends as we left for home after the service, nearly made us to decide forgoing our membership of St Mary's Church, Ijebu-Imusin. We wondered with those close to us if Jesus was only interested in the wealth of parents and that those of us poor folks have no place with him. Such was the emphasis on dress that I would have been lost to the church with two of our friends if not for the tact and care of my parents. Many Churches insist on gowns for ladies and a three piece suit for males if they were to be ushers and nothing short of the standard. The question is, must we be European in our dress to be able to collect the offering of the people and to bring it to the altar for blessing? Must we dress in a certain way before we can direct people and maintain decency in worship? Surely not! Who among us could have said that any of the Apostles ever wore a suit and tie as we know them today? The Church in Africa could copy other Churches and be receptive to the yearnings of their people by simply being an African who lives and worships the God of the entire world in Africa. Since I was collated an archdeacon, I have always run away from anything that makes me wear the cope at the Cathedral of Our Saviour in Ijebu Diocese because of the heat from the old chancel. That I preferred my simple cassock and surplice with stole within the cathedral did not reduce the efficacy of my ministry and the ministry is always effectual even when I wear any other dress. I am convinced that God looks at the heart of man not at his dress alone. As we listen and learn, we may become more aware of the prejudices we have that stereotype the poor and prevent us from being friends to the hungry and the stranger among us.

The Child Benefit

For most people in the northern hemisphere, retirement is something like an icing on the cake after years of labour. Anyone who has laboured either serving the state or family business would be entitled to a good holiday and a regular source of income in old age. Many Africans on the contrary labour until they drop dead except for the few with pensions, and unfortunately it is not always a tale of joy for many retired civil servants who could go for months without receiving pensions. Many die while awaiting their lump sum or gratuity to be paid. This is an injustice that the national government needs to change for the good of the people and many of these pensioners are also Christians. Many children in Nigeria of my time would normally assist parents to augment the family income either as trainees or hawkers, selling anything your parents could produce or cook. This enables some relief from the trauma which poverty bequeathed on a family as parents struggle to provide for the needs of the family. In the position of being the fifth child among ten children and without any government welfare or support in place, it was often very difficult to have a lost pencil replaced. I learnt at the age of nine to produce brooms and baskets for sale in the local market, and this was of massive assistance to buy the annual dress and sandals each Christmas period, as my clay-bank would be opened at that time. As a young boy, I assisted my family by selling food stuffs, 'fufu' made from fermented cassava tubers, or making brooms and baskets from palm leaves and fronds which I sold on the 5-day markets and my earnings were kept in my clay or wooden banks which were then broken near the resumption of a new school session. A good savings ensured a new school uniform or a new dress for another year. My mother was scared of raising a spoilt child, so she was a strict disciplinarian, but my father pampered me all the way. This pampering from my father did not go well with those older siblings as it complicated family relationships. Sometimes, I would be intimidated by my older siblings, as they waited for the opportunity to bully me when alone with them. My childhood involved me assisting my mother to transport the cassava tubers she bought from the farms, like a typical beast of burden, with Adesoji, my younger brother, when he could join us, we would trudge barefooted with loads of tubers on our heads. The farms were an average of about three to four miles return trip from home and there were rare days, when our mother travelled to sell her products in Lagos, we would have a well-deserved rest. This would come after going to fetch water at the stream. The nearest stream was three miles in both directions. Poor me! Most of the time I would get home with my bucket half full as movement along the rocky road and a steep and narrow path made it hard for the container to retain all the water. Sometimes, when I was nearer home I might step on a sharp pebble and there would go all my water and myself lying on the ground. I would be lucky then not to be rebuked for my negligence, playfulness and carelessness, with or without bruises. Immediately after school I would begin hawking fufu, and I would normally want to sell at least two basketfuls as I meander my way advertising along the streets and corners, encouraging my customers to buy from me at least a wrap or two of fufu. By the evening, I would be tired but this weariness could not be compared to when I had to bring in the cassava tubers from the farm a long torturous stony bush path on a hot afternoon. Anytime I attend to the children or visit any one of the three schools in the benefice, I would remember those children back in Africa who were still missing the joy of being a child and I pray "God give me the grace to do something tangible to help the huge number of children whose parents missed the joys of their childhood and whose childhood is being fleeced by their peculiar situations." It was pertinent to note that the good people of Teesdale contribute good sums of money to support Christian Aid, Water Aid and other charities from time to time to alleviate poverty in Africa and other places because kindness flows in their veins. It was part of the deal for being nice and good children to be able to support your family as not doing anything tangible meant that the family would continue to suffer; this could even be compounded if any of your parents were passing through a difficult phase of life such as ill-health or they die in their toil. Children from poorer families face greater hardship and the urgency to provide hundred per cent for their welfare which included what to wear and what to eat. In the Nigeria of my youth and until I grew up in my fifties one thing was certain, there was nothing called the child benefit, unemployment allowance, job-seekers subsidy or tax credits from the government, and everyone fended for themselves or they suffered. This of course for most of us was a school of life where willy-nilly lessons were learnt and essential life-skills were acquired, and all you could hear from us were the affirmations of positive confessions as embodied in the promises of God for His own in the Scriptures, such as 'All is well with my soul', statements that encourage and give us hope for the future.

The Neighbourhood Vigilante

One morning at Ijebu Ode in the 1990s, we woke up to learn that vigilantes had caught some armed robbers who robbed on a street during the night, and as usual jungle justice had been meted out to them. The corpses lay on the road until everyone had had the opportunity to see the faces of the robbers, perhaps they could be identified so that their family could be stigmatised. Sometimes when a person was caught stealing, that person would be led to his family home and be burnt alive with used tyres to serve as a deterrent to others, even though stealing Government officials are not seen as robbers. Some families have been excommunicated from their community for having a child whose way of life was perceived to be suspicious, as the people believe that without a wayward person in a village it would be hard if not impossible for vandals and robbers to invade such a community. The links have to be severed, and in doing this no stone was left unturned to maintain some relative peace for the community. In many communities, there were no cases of spent convictions, once there was a robbery or burglary, any thief, anyone suspected to have stolen in the past, who has associated with a criminal in one form or the other became suspects and in danger of death, unless their innocence was strenuously proved. The failure of government to provide security has left people with little option but to provide their own kind of security. But that leads to vengeance, retaliation, bitterness, hatred and malice, and an almost endless cycle of senseless violence and insecurity. Whatever type of operational system that enables jungle justice is a proof of the level into which the country has degenerated.

Any other business?

It may be important to consider the items on this Agenda as issues of Social Concern needing urgent attention in our world. Just like Jesus when he cleansed the Temple, we may need to know where we stand as a City set on the hill today.

I. Corruption and its effects

The impact of corruption as a weapon of violence on the developing countries has a catastrophic effects in my part of sub-Sahara Africa that the Church cannot afford to disregard. The Church shall be seen as part of the problem if the bastion of truth is busy solving its own problems rather than thinking of the common good. The Church had in the past actively sought from politicians, not-so-transparent businessmen and top public servants to contribute or donate into the coffers of the Church. This happens with all religions around us. Many dioceses and archdeaconries were created simply because of the request of these financial pillars for a particular area once they had pledged to support the new Diocese or Archdeaconry. The financial pillars often dictate to the Church who is to be appointed their archdeacon or bishops of the diocese. In an era where church growth is expected to be the focus, the Holy Spirit is expected to guide the Church. It remains to be seen in the future if the major criteria for the creation of such dioceses and archdeaconries are on worthy foundations. If a corrupt person who stole fifty pence from the government coffers, and silenced the religious leaders with an inappropriate donation of five pence to either the church or the mosque or to a community association, the person has deprived the society of all the amenities the fifty pence was meant to contribute such as roads, hospitals, and water. Christian morality and ethics shall not only be poorer for it but will remain the number one victim. I affirm with others who had been unequivocal on this matter that the Church in sub—Sahara Africa in which the church of Nigeria is a part needs to acknowledge its responsibilities as a transformation organ in Nigeria.

i. Disability exchange

The sheer neglect of the sick or the disabled that causes armies of disabled people to trade their disability for alms in our towns as badges of honour remained a testimony for our shame. Whatever might be said about decadence in Europe or other nations is just the tip of the ice-berg in many sub–Saharan African societies, with sexual violence and harassment the order of the day in the teacher-student relationships or male-female relationships in many areas a step lower than what is to be expected for decency. Many of the societies have no regard whatsoever for either the young ones or the females. According to popular practice, the elderly cannot possibly make a mistake. In many societies, the only person they blame are the female victims of abuse or harassment, which in actual fact is simply rubbing salt into a festering injury. The Church of Christ that prides herself as being the salt and light of the world must not be nationally intimidated, but should support the efforts of local ministers in a concerted manner with all the resources at her disposal and should not be seen only in the shadowy corridors of power. The national Churches are agents for positive change and they must remain so. Corruption is a form of violence, as the implications of corruption can only be better imagined by the civilised world, because people die daily and needlessly in many underdeveloped countries because a greedy fellow converts the funds that are meant to be used for the provision of basic amenities into personal accounts. The poverty that ensues from this situation can have effects that are better imagined. The role of the Church in any society is to stand in the gap and to tell both the governed and the government the mind of God for their situations. From the Gospels, Jesus challenges the powers that be not to put heavy yokes on the people. The case of sub-Sahara Africa is a nightmare where health care, social welfare, and public services are thin or virtually non-existent; disease and malnutrition are rampant. The road accidents are a massive problem, and the country is constantly under the power of the night marauders who also attack or even kill during the day time. In a country that has experienced much hardship, there is a danger that faith might become culturally pietistic, offering a distraction from pain and agony by making spirituality the scapegoat. Enlightened Christians with some affluence care more responsibly and assist not only their families but whoever they regard as their neighbours, but the government's role has become virtually non-existent. Where has all the money earned from exports gone and where are the budget allocations for roads, health facilities and education for generations? Or in other words what have we to show for them? Should the national churches not be in the vanguard to safeguard the interests of the oppressed and down-trodden of our societies? In this I give kudos to Abp. Desmond Tutu of Southern Africa, and to some extent retired Abp. Akinola of Nigeria, who speaks out while others seem contented to be private chaplains to the rich and powerful. We need to hold our leaders to account, and be accountable ourselves as Christians. Today, despite the national wealth of many nations in sub-Saharan Africa, the standard of living for the vast majority of people remains abysmally low. The Governments have yet to put in place the process for the welfare of the vulnerable and the poor, yet ill-gotten wealth finds its way into bank vaults overseas. It is not uncommon to see lying along a major road, people with diseased, stinking ulcers and other forms of disability to attract concerned people to give tokens or alms to enable the recipients feed daily. This should not be acceptable in this age and time. The government can step in to assist these needy people. The national Church must empathise with a situation that bred such an environment in Africa. According to Thornton 2011, 'the Archbishop's political role encompasses both participation in political debate and giving meaning to the more sacred moments of national life, such as mourning and death'. Thornton affirms the role of the Archbishop of Canterbury that 'in the area of criminal justice that the office-holders spoke about deficiencies in the existing prison system, and argued that there should be greater use of restorative or community forms of justice'. Otokiti 2011 opines that the Church in Nigeria is unwell and in need of critical change and restoration. He cited studies to show that in comparing churched and unchurched Nigerians, in matters such as cheating and fornication, there is a little difference if any, in the ethical views and behaviour of Nigerians. He concluded that 'in spite of many churches filling to capacity with some having three services on Sundays, dishonesty, stealing, bribery and corruption, armed robbery, injustice and looting of government properties are on the rise'. Could it be people other than these faithful people who are perpetrating these crimes? Many would be tempted to think that Christians in Church behave against their profession of faith while on the streets. If this is so, then we all need to mend our ways. According to Kalu 2011, child trafficking in the eastern part of

Nigeria is a lucrative trade. He cited a United Nations opinion which states that 'at least ten children are sold across Nigeria daily and the traffickers seldom caught. Even when they were caught, they easily buy their way out. Child trafficking is illegal in Nigeria and carries a fourteen year jail term on conviction. Otokiti concluded that the Church has not done enough and will do better to preach balance sermons and that Christian leaders are at a loss over the challenge of moral decadence that their faith appears unable to combat. All Christians will need to live by what they believe in the Bible and abide with God's instructions. The Church's social role and modelling remains true today and the African House of Bishops cannot stay away from contributing to the national good while the vast majority of those being led at Church level suffer untold deprivation nationally. The Church may need to repent of its role in the scandal of maladministration and poor governance in Africa and its dilatory response to administrations that wasted the country's resources, when the Church is fully aware that the blessing of God in the natural resources is the good we do with it.

ii. Domestic violence

One of the areas in which I believe that the Church in the sub-Sahara Africa should be in the vanguard is for human dignity. In the 21st century it is primitive that some men treat their women folk like second rate and wife beating is easily condoned. This is unacceptable when religious leaders are sometimes involved, and you find parishioners occasionally pleading with a pastor or Islamic cleric to settle rifts with their wives. The act of spouse beating and any form of marital or family violence has for long been crying for remedy in the global south and the Church leaders will do well to be models, fighting against the continuous abuse of our mothers and sisters. I was driving through a major city in south-west Nigeria a few months ago when I witnessed a crowd trying desperately to separate a fighting couple. Among the group of these peace makers were some who were laughing and cracking insidious jokes as they tried to block the heavy-weight husband from hitting the feather weight wife, the man with his dress torn while the woman was half-naked. The peace-makers seemed to be enjoying the spectacle as they groped the woman, pretending to be doing everything in her best interest. Both couples were being called religious names, and if our religiosity does not stop us from a show of shame, what then is our point of claiming to be religious? Strangely enough such rifts are normally left for the family to settle at home by the police when such serious fundamental rights were infringed upon, whereas such acts should be sanctioned. There is a strong need by the Church to protect the women folks from abuse. The Church must stand with all the oppressed. All forms of sexual and gender abuse must be sanctioned. Can the Church look again at the rate of domestic and sexual violence from among her ranks and seek to formulate safeguards to protect both adults and children? I am conscious of the different disciplinary measures that are in place to deal with the priests when they misbehave, what about when it is within the laity or when it involves a Bishop. There is more to be done, a sense of unfinished tasks, more so as the Church keeps marching on. Misunderstanding, mistrust, disagreements, anger and jealousy, can hinder mutual feelings of love and confidence. Married couples should be cautious of anger as a dangerous emotion which is not predictive of marital understanding but that good communication increases marital joy in the relationship. It is also observed from casual observations that there was a direct relationship between positive personal interactions and companionship. This shows that the level of communication is related to positive marital interactions. Communication in marriage however is not just a total disclosure of oneself. This is in addition to that an ongoing process of sharing thoughts and feelings openly and fearlessly. This includes hostile feelings towards others which should be shared; but in a good relationship they are shared with appropriate apologies and an appeal for help in getting rid of them; and that makes all the difference. It is also observed that happily married couples are more likely to involve a female partner who has a well-modulated voice. Adesanya 2000 surveyed 260 wives in south west Nigeria, out of which 96 (37%) were dissatisfied with the companionship received from their husbands, 124 (42 %) were satisfied while 40 (15%) of the wives who fill Questionnaires were very pleased with their spouses affection. There is considerable support for the proposition that socio-economic status is positively related to the maintenance of the marriage institution. Cutright (1971) hypothesed that Money is the major source of husband-wife disagreement. This observation appear to be consistent with what can be casually observed in many Nigerian societies where low income from husband usually lead to spousal frustrations as to how to cater to feed and educate their children and where non-availability of funds create marital tension among the spouses. Accordingly Adesanya 2002, showed that there is a positive relationship between economic well-being and marital stability among couples. Presence of economic well-being in particular was major source of husband-wife harmony. This shows that spouses with economic well-being more often enjoy marital stability than poverty prone couples or couples who take credit facilities for daily survival. This could affirm that comfortable couples were more concerned with psychological and emotional interaction; while the poor partners saw as more urgent in their lives resolution of financial problems and unstable physical actions of their partners. Adesanya further asserts that the major reason why economic well-being is the overall strongest predictor of marital stability among couples may be because of her institutional nature. The fulfillment of those areas of institutional marriage such as provision of residence, food and other such needs for the family is based on economic well-being. It can however be argued that economic well-being is a major platform from which a lot of other major factors can be provided. On this economic platform many spouses then hope to be provided emotional resources such as gentleness and affection. Mature men meet adjustment to getting older with an understanding and calm acceptance without escapism. Sometimes, spouses respond violently and very often with negative reactions to the extra-marital affair situation, which deepens and makes it very difficult to repair and rebuild the relationship. Some spouses lose self-control and in a fit of anger destroy or maim the goose that lays the golden eggs, smear their personalities. In a culture full of superstitions and witchcraft, spouses and their relatives may go for the witch doctor asking him to help send away the offending girl friend or concubine. Marital partners must live peaceably.

iii. Ethnic and tribal prejudice

Perhaps it is time to add another question to job application forms or the national census forms to know those within national demography, whose three generations have been living on a particular area with none of their families ever moving out. From Biblical times with the immediate children of Adam and Eve through to Abraham and as to the 10th till the 16th century Europe, all the way to the Americas for both blacks and whites, in the creation of modern day China and Asia to the communities of Africa and Oceanic, migration has always been a challenge. It is as much a challenge in Africa as it is to other continents of the world. Most of the chaos and the unending violence in present day Nigeria is attributable to movement of people and land ownership, and just as it was in Southern Africa and other places. It appears immigration is discussed as a fall-guy item to cover administrative and economic failures. Is it not the panacea topic or the magic wand to be used to solve all the economic woes of the nations? Yes, countries like Ghana and Nigeria were tempted in the past to expel immigrants among them to their own peril. No nation has made it economically without the huge inputs of their nationals home and abroad and the new nationals they have assimilated. The more I think of the early explorers such as the Normans, British, Spanish, Chinese or the Portuguese and their exploits in many countries of the world, it has become obvious that despite all the claims to negative intentions, immigration has brought the world closer to each other and a higher degree of civilisation is brought forward. Is it not also responsible for the metropolitan status of many cities across the globe today in the creation of a new world? The more integration and social mobility we have in this world, the clearer it becomes that where your parents were born, your religion or the colour of your skin or eyes, or your body size shall not matter rather what shall matter will be the ability to reason, use skills, give and receive love. In

Nigeria, ethnic prejudice was expressed for example in the Junkun-Tiv age old conflict in Taraba and Benue states and the Itshekiri-Ijaw conflict in Delta State. Within the South Western Nigeria, the Ife-Modakeke or Ilaje-Arugbo Ijaw conflicts in both Osun and Ondo State created despair for family and marital relations. Will being a spouse from the south of the South Western Nigeria for example being an Ijebu or Egba spouse or from the north of the South Western Nigeria for example being an Oyo or Akoko spouse or on the other hand being a spouse married to the South Western Nigeria from an area outside the South Western Nigeria contribute to marital stability? Are there special norms or belief of certain ethnic groups within the South Western Nigeria that contribute to or endanger the marital stability among couples? Sedmak (2001) observes the history of researching ethnically mixed marriages is dominated by the studies of the interpersonal relationships. Sedmak further observed that sociological studies on ethnic differentials evidently lack qualitative research on interethnic relations with an emphasis on the interpersonal relationship. This contribution presented intimate interpersonal relations and subtle personal circumstances. Because of its basic features that distinguish this approach efforts were made as to collections of ethnically mixed marriages as a specific form of intercultural encounters on the interpersonal level of partnership. I can assume that raised voices on immigration may be a panic button to remind individuals of their insecurity in the light of dwindling economic and cultural resources? Some are scared of others taking up jobs even when the jobs have never been there in the first instance, and all you need is for an immigrant to create a job. There are many immigrants who are not economic immigrants but pay their rent, buy their houses and buy their comfort from funds brought in from overseas. Yes, there are immigrants who abuse the generosity of their hosts and refuse to integrate or are criminally-minded, these are identifiable and need to be treated as the law of the land permits. Also there are other categories of immigrants who make business possible for economic growth. Rarely will you hear those who purchase multi-million premier football clubs referred to as non-EU immigrants or those who establish shops and restaurants as people who duly pay taxes and contribute to the economy.

It remains a fact that the mature can welcome others that are different from them and notice the quality of the value that has been added to culture and economy. It is therefore with dismay that I view the comments and the antagonism especially of some African church leaders who intend to ostracise their congregations from the rest of the world. The European continent is generally receptive to immigrants trying to find relevance in their adopted homes, even with a supermarket tag of categories such as EU or non-EU, workers. The reality is that due to modern day social and economic mobility, people move across geographical boundaries given the fact that transportation and technology have helped to make the world a global village. The people make every effort to escape into any place that gives them better satisfaction and prospects. In an attempt to achieve economic emancipation, the educated middle-class, the courageous with the spirit of adventure and the novo rich were able to move across borders whatever their race or creed. The need for freedom and security remains a driving force. It appears strange that the children of people who stick gold in other people's backyard without an invitation now agitate and harass the offspring of the land from which they got their wealth for the effrontery of becoming their manual workers. Of course, it is not what people didn't know about the immigrant that is the problem, but what people thought they knew. On the other hand, Pincus and Ehrlich (1999) observed that although discrimination has decreased overall yet prejudice—motivated interactions have increased and expressions of prejudice have shifted from biological inferiority to cultural differences. Some other people reject the classifications of certain ethnic groupings contending that both negative and positive human characteristics are embedded in all people notwithstanding the ethos of such an ethnic group or sub-culture. They observe that individuals must be treated on his or her own merit without any bias as to the ethnicity or the sub-group of the person and therefore reject the social system that classifies one as strangers or as natives. It is simply the fact that some people have an attitude that derives from the time before the advent of William Wilberforce and they have to be persuaded from taking the whole human race back into the dark ages. It appeared racial prejudice is not as dead as some people believed. It is everywhere in various degrees, and still to some extent indulged by all people across the world, but that does not make it acceptable. It is sad to note that tribal prejudice is still widespread in many areas of Nigeria and across Africa of the 21st century. However, some of us who have read and noticed the overall effects of the do-gooders on the European societies might have the tendency to believe that this ugly practice of racial prejudice is gone for good in Europe and in the entire world. The isolated experience mentioned in this book, exceptional as it were, is not the norm, as most people in Teesdale are kind hearted, loving and above all politically correct and conscious of the sensibilities and sensitivity of other peoples' feelings. Yet a moment of madness from an individual can create the wrong impression. The examples in this book, showed that more needs to be done by way of public enlightenment and education. What can you say in a situation when a man says to you openly and clearly, ' I don't want you to touch me' and goes away from you to shake hands with others. This also showed that despite civilisation, developments and all the efforts and gains of the past to combat inequality, prejudice and intolerance there are still pockets of people who are still living in the dark past. The exposure and maturity displayed by the enlightened heart is helpful. This perhaps reflected in the interactions with the youth and many people. Even the mentioned unpleasant encounters were isolated events. One finds a level of understanding and exposure among people that appeared more urban than those expected of those who inhabit the rural areas, because of the possible multi-cultural interactions. However, surprisingly many city dwellers might have a narrow view of life whereas many rural folks have global view and are welcoming, receptive and unbiased. I look back to situations in sub-Sahara Africa and the country of my birth in particular where the different tribes do not freely mix to the extent of calling a different region outside their language group home, and where no matter how long a southerner had lived in the North and vice-versa, he or she will still be referred to as a stranger, with consequent emotional and tribal prejudice. In every incident that I witnessed, however, it was to the credit of the English people that they felt disturbed and did everything possible to make me feel at home and welcome. They dealt with the situation, and all I could do is to show gratitude for their friendly disposition and understanding. No single person has openly defended anyone who has passed a politically incorrect comment. Today, in Europe it appears racial prejudice has become a thing of the past or grossly non-existent, and that whatever colour you are or race does not matter; because racial prejudices has long been considered unacceptable in any civilised society. Yes, there is no country of the world in this century that has racism as a state policy, and it must be an on-going education to ensure that individuals that were pushing us back to that ignoble age were made to imbibe the issues involved in social justice. The assumption is that personal qualities of merit and skills outweigh racial considerations. More so there is legislation in place to promote and protect equal opportunities, racial justice and harmony. According to the Church of England, there are many ethnic minority priests within the Church of England alone, and there are encouragements by the different Diocesan Directors of Ordination to make their numbers rise even further. They continue to give all encouragement for the ministry of all in the Church. More so as with God, there is no colour or tribal barriers as all people are equal before their God. Let us comfort ourselves with the words of Joshua 1.9 *'Be strong and courageous. Do not be terrified; do not be discouraged, for the LORD your God will be with you wherever you go"* and the parting words of Jesus in Matthew 28.20 saying *"Surely, I am with you always, to the very end of the age".*

A national malaise

I noticed a large gathering of men gathered under a tree, joking and laughing during a Diocesan Synod in 2006. These gatherings of able young men have always been a feature during the Synod each year and adequate preparations were normally made to care for them. This situation is not peculiar to Church gatherings alone but it is a normal phenomenon during conferences and social engagements. When I was at Italupe, I had a personal driver, and certain other staff because that was the norm, but personal security implications and good management of resources has proved that this is not a good practice. Many public officials in Europe, the priests and Bishops will certainly drive their cars to the length and breadth of their dioceses and beyond, and you will be surprised that people as old as 86 years old may drive their own cars. It is not illegal to employ any personal staff, but you will need to pay the person at least the national minimum wage and consider good practices. In Africa and in Nigeria, many domestic staff were under-paid and under-employed. I strongly believe that this was part of the legacy left to Africans from colonial days. The European in colonial days would normally hire full-time drivers for each car, cooks, house-maids, gate-keeper, gardeners, messengers, and domestic day and night security guards. When the white colonial officers left, the indigenous African officers that took over from them continued in these practices. Today there are an array of hangers-on in the home of one who barely takes care of his family, and many who are able to buy a second-hand imported car from Europe or America employs a driver. The car owner wants to employ a full-time driver for a car that has been used for many years by previous owners. While the car is being driven by this employee, the owner of the car will seat on the back seat which has been designated the owner's corner. This is despite the fact that this 'owner' only leaves from his/her house to the shop or office and return home. Meanwhile the driver does nothing for most of the day. What is the job description for the drivers, office-messengers, house-maids, gatemen and the like which we employ other than it being an ego-enhancing trip? Is it not for ever true that the devil finds work for the idle hand? What is the implication of the army of idle hands that we create for today and the future? When anyone who is grossly underpaid and doing a work where he is grossly under-employed as a full-time worker, with the luxury of having nothing to do except to imagine how his/her boss spends money, will this not have national implications? Is it not time that we raise the awareness that people need to learn how to drive and be willing to do so, if they intend to own a car, or that they must provide a good pay and job description for domestic workers to avoid abuse. We must start a campaign to abolish the class system within our society that is already yielding dangerous dividends.

Chapter Five

In the Church of England

Diocese of Southwark.

During the periods of my stay between 2004 until 2006 and from 2007 on a consistent manner, I have always worshipped at St. Matthew's Church at Elephant and Castle, London where Rev. Neil served as the incumbent, a wonderful man in whose veins the milk of kindness flows. At St. Matthew's, an inner-city multi-cultural parish, Rev. Roy Dorey and I assisted both the Rector and people from a range of cultural backgrounds. I arrived London, met with my son—Adeolu, and set off for the United States of America to unwind. After a month, I returned to London and I set on with the task of mending my health and for one and a half years, I was selling my stock and shares in Nigeria to support my rent and fend for myself, yet at that time it was being rumoured that I was planning to ditch ministry or the church. At this point, God was reminding me of the universality of the Church and that He Jesus is Immanuel; 'God with me', he is present everywhere and could be worshiped anywhere and at any time. I must have spent thousands of pounds sterling and millions of Naira to sustain myself even though the Nigerian church paid my salary for some months after my departure which was a help before they stopped. Without the right atmosphere and means of working in the UK, it was the Grace of God and the help of God's people that comforted me during this trial of living. To compound the issues it was at this time that the sales of my stock and shares which I have always used to pay for my sustenance and accommodation witnessed a crash during the global recession. To me it was as if the forces of nature and economic forces were staging a coup against me, more so when I did not have any other means of livelihood but the power of God teaching me His gracious principles sustained me. All this while, I was assisting Rev. Neil McKinnon as honorary Assistant priest at St. Matthew at the Elephant and Castle in London, and I had always worshipped in this Church since I was introduced to the Church by Nike in 2004 whenever I was in London. Bishop Butler through the recommendation of Bishop Christopher with the prompting of Neil facilitated the necessary permissions. My fiftieth birthday in 2007 while I was in London was wonderfully celebrated in meditation, alone with my God. In finding relief for my medical problem, I had been privileged to have some of the best in the land attend to me. The cost was enormous but the results massive. I had let it known to my family that I would love to be alone to review my life and think things through, with neither special menu nor singing. My sisters' in-law—Bolaji and Yetunde devised a means to celebrate with me. Just two days before my birthday, Bolaji mentioned the need for an urgent meeting to solve a family problem. It was a trap I walked into, two days after my birthday. I went to Gravesend, Kent to solve a family problem not realising it was my surprise birthday party. Having walked into it, I simply enjoyed it, danced and dined. As time passed after the letter of appointment from Bishop John Parker into the Diocese of Ripon and Leeds, Neil's personality continued to unfold. Neil was such a pleasant person and a blessed character. A man who would not boast about his achievements but whose outlook stretched for miles and miles in all directions. He is the model of a human rights activist and fights against all forms of rights abuse and prejudice. Neil, who as rector of St. Matthew, Elephant and Castle, under whom I served as a non-stipendiary honorary assistant priest had shown an interest in my medical and financial situations and gave all the support which he could possibly render. As a Christian counsellor he showed concern and cared for my family as a caring, kind father and minister of the Gospel would do. Rev Neil made all the preparations for my send-off, bought a series of books that he knew as a priest would be of good and regular use for me in ministry. He also gave pieces of advice and prayed for my family. The service was followed by a reception where guests and the congregation were entertained. It was a generous and lavish party and everyone had enough to drink and eat and if wanted to take away. When he spoke of giving me a send-off during the Easter day service of 2009, it had a personal note to it. It was an emotional farewell, which was in recognition that even though he wanted me to get a position as an incumbent in the Church of England, he believed going up to the North East of England was a risky proposition and too great an adventure. The minority ethnic population was less than 0.1%, "how would I cope" he enquired? He was concerned that the accent of the north-east and especially of the North-Yorkshire people and county Durham being so different to that of Londoners and of the south east England. This was a major concern to him. To him and others who feared that I might get into some form of harm, it was unimaginable. St. Matthew bade me farewell on Easter day, barely two weeks before my departure from London and I was treated to a 'This is your Life' presentation, with words of affection, appreciation, goodwill, gifts and prayers. It was a moving spectacle as I was humbled by the show of love and the generosity of Neil and St. Matthews Parochial Church Council (PCC). However, from this point onwards, I was becoming anxious on the progress of living, as what I was hearing and noticed from the on-going relationship between the provinces of the Anglican Communion were giving me some concern. The reasons for my anxiety were due largely to two factors. First, it appeared that candidates over fifty years of age were not being encouraged to apply for first time stipendiary ministry. Secondly, it appeared that priests were not being encouraged to move from non-stipendiary to stipendiary positions, and all sorts of excuses ranging from the discriminatory to the ridiculous were being adduced for their refusal, and some minority ethnic clergy were suspicious of intentions. I did not belong to any of the two groups. I was not just getting into ministry, and have never been a part-time priest in all my life, but one who felt abandoned due to ill-health. It was with great joy that I served in Southwark and to experience the reception and accommodation of the diocese of Ripon and Leeds under the leadership of Bishops John and James, without any prejudice whatsoever. Not exactly knowing what to expect, but God must have led me to Teesdale by the way and manner fellowship was built across the Diocese.

The Diocese of Ripon & Leeds

In the Province of Nigeria, the Diocesan Bishop publishes a list every June or/and December of those located into their first appointments and those transferred from Church A to Church B. The Churches then accept the postings while those who object for various reasons, make representations to the Bishop. It is assumed it is the Bishop's prerogative to locate and transfer his clergy. Apart from the issue of The Common Tenure which comes into effect for most Bishops and clergy at the Church of England in January 2011, here the wardens or the church representatives along with their respective PCCs decide what manner of man or woman lead their Churches and are actively involved in the selection and appointment process. In the Church of England the priests are in a sense called to serve the churches, and this is not a process left to any one person, as the PCCs, senior staff, the national Church and Bishop of each diocese were involved at any particular stage. Therefore the first phase of the interview was with first panel headed by the area Dean of Richmond deanery who also supervised the two Benefices during the period of interregnum and whose administrative geographical deanery is much larger than three or four dioceses put together in many countries. The first panel consisted of a full-bred Englishman from Liverpool and with a vision of the larger picture of the Church, who in his younger days spent his gap year in Sierra Leone teaching as he still kept good memories of his stay in Freetown area. He was the Deanery chair. Apart from the Deanery chair were wardens and representatives from each church. Their opinions and contributions matter and they have to be satisfied about any choice. They constituted with the Deanery chair, the first panel of interviewers. The next stage of the interview was with a panel consisting of the Deanery lay chair,—a lady who was a former Mayor of the rich and ancient town of Richmond, an astute politician and administrator; a firm and disciplined elder and Reader in Richmondshire, also present was the Venerable Archdeacon of Richmond Archdeaconry who retired from a flourishing nursing career to come into the full ministry of the church, and later to become one of the very first lady archdeacons in the northern province of York, in the Church of

England. A chat with her during the short break between the two interviews confirmed why she was so much loved by all and sundry as an effective minister of the Gospel; a lady with a caring and cheerful disposition to duty. She came across as someone full of warmth and compassion and aware of the relationship between integrity and the ministry. She had a global view of the world around her. I was later informed that her parents had once lived in Ghana many years ago. The Diocesan Bishop presided over the second interview. Watching and listening to the Bishop and realising where I was coming from, background, culture and various experiences in ministry, I marvelled at the humility of the Bishop, and how very loving and positively different, he manifested to me a refreshing presence of a Christian leader, a humble bishop. This man is a shepherd of the flock under whom I should be happy to serve. The events following this contact with him and later his wife Barbara confirmed to us my original assessment of John the Bishop. A senior member in the House of Bishops and a leading light in the House of Lords, a man who championed through his teachings the welfare of those whom society would have criminalised for their effrontery to escape the doom of poverty, violence, and other natural catastrophes of their native lands—the immigrants! As a mark of his humility, I had never seen any piece of diocesan information where John had been referred to as the Lord Bishop of Ripon and Leeds, yet those who were never members of any county council or ever held political offices in their countries on becoming bishops assumed the title of 'Lord Bishop'. The Deanery had also made arrangements for me to visit all the churches that would be in my care. The retired Reverend Peter, who incidentally was to become my neighbour, and who eventually shared the ministry with me and others was given this task, to drive me round and he did it beautifully. He showed me the places of interest from village to village until we returned to Barnard Castle to have a quiet lunch. I was transferred to the care of Revd Haworth and enjoyed classical music which Kathryn, his wife played in their house. On the evening of 14th January 2009, returning from the interview and in the house of the Deanery chair in Aldbrough, I was informed through Archdeacon Janet that the panel of interviewers from the Benefice of Romaldkirk with Cotherstone and Laithkirk, and the

Benefice of Startforth, united with Rokeby with Boldron, and Brignall and Bowes had accepted me as their next Priest in Charge, to guide the two separate Benefices towards becoming a united or joint one. There was a point in time in which all the churches had their own separate priests and the Rectors of Romaldkirk with Cotherstone had also been afforded the title, Lord of the Manor. Those who heard the news were petrified at the daunting challenges, concerned about the Church services, the rota and the increasing demand of the villages. Yet, I was thrilled and happy that this was a challenge worth embarking upon and this was a mission for Christ. I started to look forward to working in collaboration and with the cooperation from the Churches and to visualise where God would be leading us. However, coming from the Nigerian end of the Church as part of the world wide Anglican communion, I thought things would move fast, but this was not to be. The Criminal Records Bureau check took about six weeks, I had to just wait while the police national records and other records were checked to detect if I had any previous convictions of abuse with either children or vulnerable adults. Then there was the need to apply for the Archbishop of York's licence to be able to officiate in the province of York, and for this the necessary applications were made by me, despite the fact that I held the Licence of the Archbishop of Canterbury. The Diocesan Bishop must ensure that all these processes were successfully completed before any formal announcement of the appointment could be made, first within the parishes where I would serve, and nationally in the press. Immediately I got the Criminal Records Bureau (CRB) clean report from Venerable Peter Burrow's (now Bishop of Doncaster) office in Leeds, my Letter of Appointment was sent by the diocesan Bishop. It was also a legal requirement for me to formally accept the offer of appointment. This was strange to me, as I could never recollect writing a Letter accepting the offer to minister in any Church prior to this as Letters of Location and Transfers were seen as routine letters. On receipt of my letter of acceptance I was invited by the area Dean to come up to Barnard Castle again to have a quick look at the houses and to make a choice. This choice was made easy as the Diocese had a focus of expectation for the proposed united Benefices. We arrived at Startforth on May 1st 2009 and I was licensed and installed on May 20th 2009 and while I was finding it a little hard to keep with the pace, I was made to understand that "some things take time", and that "it was a process" not an event. During the time between arriving and being installed we were not allowed to worship in any of the Churches within the two Benefices. One Sunday morning, my wife and I were to take a bus ride to Darlington from Barnard Castle. On this day I learnt what was to become a major principle for my ministry in Teesdale. Even though we were the first to arrive at the bus stop we realised that the next four persons to arrive after us were elderly, and we requested that they enter the bus ahead of us, out of respect, but they turned us down. In unison they chorused, as if they had rehearsed it time and time again, they said "no rushing, no rushing". Yes, that was a good lesson to have started from, as rushing was part of my upbringing. In the Nigerian church, some priests could accept to be in three or four services on a certain day, starting with a church with the first hymn, reading the second lesson in another Church, rushing to preach in the third Church and saying the benediction in the fourth Church. No, I would not be rushing around in Teesdale, I enthused to myself. The ministry which I subsequently started in Teesdale from May, 2009 has the propensity to become the "rushing" of a gust of wind, but every time I recollected the chorus of those elderly 'wise' women to me I always knew that the Holy Spirit of God had guided their mouths to alert and warn me to be careful and remain focussed. There must be time for reflection and meditation, the word of God must be allowed to do His work and prayers must be said with humility and therefore, "no rushing". Since then, my trips on the green Bus No. 75 or 76 have become for me a spiritual journey. While often passing through Staindrop, or Winston, Gainford, and Piercebridge into Darlington I am reminded of the enormous spiritual gifts that God has indeed deposited into the hearts of the elderly people who often constituted the bulk of co-passengers except when I travel during the time when the students and workers are on the Bus. Just about a month before our resumption, I took the decision to travel to Aldbrough St John, and setting out at 8.15pm with my wife who graciously travelled with me on that particular night despite all the odds. At one point I veered out of the motorway into a restaurant for rest and relaxation, but on our way to re-join the motorway, we nearly lost our lives, when a fast moving truck from an unexpected direction nearly collided with us. That spectacular and miraculous escape is an event I shall never forget. My lower limbs began to shake uncontrollably out of panic and I was deep down in my heart, scared of continuing the trip, but was too scared of turning back to London. I knew if at that time I mentioned it to Buki that I wanted to turn back, she would be highly pleased, and therefore I tried to be brave, even though at this time I felt like a baby wanting to weep. It was a journey of faith, life and this danger that was eager to turn our joy into sadness, but as my father would say, '*never give up because of any bad moments, because no matter how long it takes, that moment shall pass away*'. This seems parallel to the old English proverb that says '*the night is darkest when the dawn is nigh*'. As all the allowances from the Diocese had arrived and good money spent on essential commodities and having contacted and allowed the removal van to depart ahead of us to Barnard Castle we set out into the Diocese of Ripon and Leeds.

The Rectory

Welcoming visitors into our home as they kept streaming in to visit was quite a joy, sitting for some time and mentioning their names and places where they came from, it took me quite a while before I could identify those places later. Everyone who cared came to say "Hello!" and introduce themselves, some leaving behind tell-tale snaps or anecdotes that gave me cause for caution as my new ministry enfolded. It was a challenge from the very beginning. Many cards came from our Baptist, United Reformed Church, Methodist brethren and from the community who welcomed us into our new home. Yes, the new home is ours, unlike the Nigerian Church; the incumbent owns everything in a Rectory or vicarage, except the building. He or she is responsible for his life, but in the Nigerian Church, plates, furniture, cars, beddings, pots, stove or cookers, fans or air—conditioners were provided by the local Church and the priest is only responsible for the safe keeping and the cleanliness of the environment.

However, the priest in the UK receives good help in equipping himself from the Church Commissioners and help from the PCC for re-decorations. Whichever way you look at it, the Church of England in safe-guarding the wellbeing of the vicar, does not act in an intrusive manner. Sometimes in Nigeria, there is a power tussle between the vicar and people's warden or the PCC as to who would be responsible for the different aspects of a parsonage, but everyone within the Church of England knows their limit in this regard. This might be because the guidelines in the Nigerian Church are vague; some sections of the regulations were copied from the Church of England but without the priest's independence. The Diocese of Ripon and Leeds had ensured that the bungalow was clean and neat, which includes the beautiful gardens. The house that went with the job was at Startforth. It was stop-gap accommodation that was provided for the last house-for-duty priest who managed the benefice of Startforth with Brignall and Bowes, the rectories at both parishes of Startforth and for Bowes having been sold to pave the way for a new benefice. There was also a rectory at Romaldkirk which the people of Romaldkirk with Cotherstone hoped that I would occupy, as in fact they were not happy that the rectory had been left unoccupied for over three years. Some of the residents wanted the rectory to be leased to overcome the darkness in that patch of the village every night, but the diocese was keeping the house as a safety-gap in case something went wrong with their rectory arrangements in Startforth. Being a priest in charge of seven Churches strewn across many communities, with two houses to choose from, a detached bungalow and the other a standard rectory, the diocesan strategic plan was for the priest to live in Startforth as this is nearer to Barnard Castle where most of the shops and secondary schools are located and is closer to the two Church of England schools within the benefice. The ministry of other priests and readers within the benefice helped significantly to consolidate ministry in many areas as they brought a lot of variety to the churches. My administrative assistant did most of my office work which quite released me to be the priest rather than an administrator to avoid spending time flipping through files and writing letters. Most of my time therefore outside the office is used in developing friendship evangelism across the benefice, being able to chat and to share the Christian witness one on one. I had more time for prayers with my parishioners, and counselling, being the parson for the communities and among them. In my third year when plans to build a standard rectory in Startforth did not happen, the Diocese purchased a house at Cotherstone which is centrally located within the two Benefices as the new rectory.

Retreat Opportunities

The Clergy Reading week, Diocesan Training programmes, personal retreats, regular Days—off and the Annual Deanery chapter retreat came in useful. These programmes in different ways ensured my survival. Most of the time it was these programmes of retreat that provided the much needed space and discipline that enabled me to rediscover myself and kept burnout at arm's length. During these periods, the thoughts and reflections, addresses, walking in the beautiful English countryside, group discussions, generously served food, good sleep without the telephone ringing, and above all the space for listening and silence were what renewed my soul and body and kept me sane. The Clergy Reading Week at Parcevall Hall assisted greatly. I was the only priest from Ripon and Leeds diocese who teamed up with sixteen others from Bradford diocese at Parcevall Hall in Appletreewick, Skipton in 2010. "Parcevall hall, was once the home of Sir William Milner, offers guests a unique experience of hospitality in its tranquil and unrivalled setting in Upper Wharfedale. The Hall, once a farmhouse, dating back to at least 1584, was restored and extended with vision and sensitivity between the wars. The attractive gardens were laid out at the same time. On Sir William's death in 1960, Parcevall was bequeathed to Our Lady of Walsingham. It was leased to the Diocese of Bradford and a new wing was added in memory of Sir William. Sufficient accommodation was then available for the Hall to open in 1963 as a retreat and conference house." I was very grateful to the Ripon and Leeds diocese for providing the funding for this programme, without which it would not come easier. The reading week did have something for every one of us—time devoted to reading, to quiet worship, rest, walking through the woods and far enough away to ensure you come out of the place refreshed. Secondly, at other times, I have visited some retreat centres and monasteries for the art of silence and meditation, notable among them is the Friary of St. Francis in the quiet and austere port town of Alnmouth in Northumberland on the edge of the North Sea. The bell that chimed in the hallway and the sombre atmosphere and the historicity of the building was a major attraction for me. It seemed to me that God prepared the original owner of the castle to build it to taste so that it can serve God's kingdom in later years and to draw others into the faith when it mattered most. The structure appeared to have been commissioned by an ecclesiastical architect and the simplicity and all the maintenance done by the brothers over the years in their simple brown cassock; reinforced the presence of God in that humble habitation. Knocking on the door of the Friary and feeling the sense of being welcomed into the peace of God, by a friar in his habit is so different to the fuss that other Retreat houses may parade. The Deanery Chapter Retreat at The Friary of St. Francis of Assisi at Alnmouth in Northumberland is an annual event, and it helped me rest for a while and enable me to become rejuvenated in that idyllic and peaceful surroundings of the Northumberland coast of the North Sea. As a place of regular prayers and worship, walking along the beach, it also allowed me the grace of further spiritual exploration by listening to God. I have been blessed in receiving the ministry of the Friars at Alnmouth, as I have participated in the reading and the meditation on the word of God, in the prayers which the brothers lead three times daily and in the daily Eucharist. The sense of ministry which I received there helped reduce to the minimum any burn-out, emotional stress or pressure of work which could be overbearing or overwhelming to me previously. We all pray for the peace of God which surpasses all human understanding, and which comes only from God and which the world cannot give, but being present during the silent hours in the Friary, there was a tendency to experience peace, which was helped by my inability to receive the mobile phone signal, therefore a unique quality of silence was obtained. The service at the table at breakfast which was taken in silence and the way the food was served and blessed reflected what anyone might hope for in the family Eucharist as a place where love was shared and obtained. The greater part of the lessons from there centred on their simplicity; we ate at long wooden tables in the dining hall, there was a kitchen, and the monks took turns to serve and probably to prepare the meals and lead the devotions in the Chapel. The meals too were simple but graciously satisfying. The pattern of living which I noticed among the Franciscan brothers was indeed a challenge to me and would have been considered as a way of life for me if not for the age and marital situation, for those above the age of fifty were no longer encouraged to join and those with existing marriages would have no place in the brotherhood. However, their humility and simplicity of service which every Christian can aspire to have were on display for others to emulate. Today, places like The Friary of St. Francis help us to look as in a mirror to what the standards of brotherhood we have as opposed to the self-indulgence, prejudice and avarice which so much occupies the world stage and impinges on our spirituality and how far from our selves we need to move on our road back to regeneration.

The Confirmation Service.

The Confirmation service is a rite of passage into spiritual maturity. It is at confirmation that the full service of our baptism is concluded with the benediction, when the child confesses it with his or her own mouth the faith of Christ crucified and risen. It has always been a celebration of adulthood in the church as the confirmed receive Holy Communion and were qualified to hold any position within the church. The confirmation service also enables those present in the service to re-affirm their faith, and to renew their vows before God, their commitment to serve, trust and to love God and others. The Confirmation services I hosted in Romaldkirk and Bowes reminded me of my own confirmation. It was not possible for me to forget the day I was confirmed by Bishop Seth Kale in 1972. What I remembered from my confirmation service was not the sermon but the last minute procedure and rehearsal that threatened to disqualify my candidacy. The Bishop's final test was to know those of us who had our personal Bibles and Hymn books with us. Most of us fulfilled the third criterion of putting on a white robe. Some of us were wearing borrowed robes for that service, and everything in the catechisms had been well rehearsed and learnt by heart. My brother and I who were confirmed at that service were sharing between us our father's Hymn books, but as students we had our own personal Bibles as the Bible had always been one of the recommended books each student must have in the secondary school. That day we were lined up to be inspected by the Bishop, and the Bishop soon realised that I did not have my Hymn book as my father's hymn book was with my brother. I was sent out, to await the Confirmation service another time. I arrived home weeping and wailing, to meet my father who was about to mount and ride his shining white Raleigh bicycle specially washed and polished for this special occasion. My father quickly went about the business of assisting me with a borrowed Hymn book from one of his friends and I was able to make the service for which much preparation had been made. John, the diocesan Bishop and James his suffragan Bishop who conducted the first two Confirmation services in the two Benefices are both humble and pleasant personalities. The Bishops in the Church of England portray humility in speech and action, and you only needed to come close to most of them to learn the personality of Jesus. The ministry is so ordered in England that Bishops never forget that even though they are consecrated into the episcopate their priesthood and diaconate ministry is not removed from them. They are independent beings who can drive their own cars, wear their robes and treat their priests as mission partners. The ministry in the local Church is in every sense truly *'mine and yours'*. The Bishops in the diocese of Ripon and Leeds provide the leadership that I found quite reassuring. It is always a pleasure to seek their opinions on those things that matter and, whenever convenient to share a good laugh.

THE Parish Share

There was a Church that I so much treasured and I used to visit this church just to relax around the building because of the serene environment as it was a cooler place to be alone and for prayers and meditation. The church was facing a financial crunch as she could not pay her parish share that arose due to an historic error they committed with the wrong annual worshipping congregation number they had sent to the Diocese in the past years. Some were of the erroneous view that the parish share is a form of tax which the national church levied on the local parishes in order for the national Church to meet her internal and external obligations. To others, the parish share is a form of annual subscription that the local Church needed to pay to remain a member or part of the national Church. In countries such as Nigeria, the parish share is also known as "an annual assessment". The parish share was definitely not a tax; it is a contribution willingly borne by the churches to help the national church play her part both to the local churches nationally and also fulfils her external obligations. In the last few decades within the UK the parish shares have variously been called common fund or quota. Within the Church of England and in other lands, the parish share had been a matter for disputes among different congregations both for and against the payments. PCCs members even though were not ignorant of the need for the payments, often felt the need to solve all their financial problems—and there are many—before payment to the national kitty. Many PCCs also have a wrong perception as to think that if the payment is for the payment of their clergy, what is the national Church doing with the excess after their clergy have been paid? The parish share is actually a local share of each PCC contribution to ministry generally either in terms of mission or maintenance of structures, and the world wide fellowship of which clergy stipend and pension is a percentage. Therefore every PCC had an ethical and spiritual responsibility for paying it promptly. According to Osborne 2004, '*parish share is not about paying for what we get. It is about working together and sharing resources. The parish is part of a Diocese, a bigger unit, hence the need to support each other; therefore contributing our parish share is acting as if you are part of the diocese while reluctance or refusal to pay make you act as if you are not part of the diocese*'. Having thought that I had escaped from the issues of payment of Church assessments in Nigeria which was quite debilitating as financial payments to the Diocese became a major concern of the priests and I least expected any distraction in the form of parish share in the Church of England. Yet the Church must be financed to be maintained. Some village churches were particularly vulnerable to financial paucity while some enjoyed a financial health which had been made possible by bequests which might be centuries old. There was a time in the past when there was very high church attendance in the villages. That was when agrarian farming was practiced and there were many farm labourers who in obedience to the land-owner would be seated and present in Church, or as the case in Teesdale when lead miners would be in numbers in the Church before today's level of industrialisation changed all that. Today, there were fewer people in the Church as lead mining has virtually evaporated and a Combine Harvester machine would do today the work of 100 farm labourers. This change led to so many changes in the Church and also in the distribution of the clergy among the villages. It was expected that the shared clergy could only be thinly present on the ground and getting to know the congregation in a meaningful way might be randomly achieved. Sometimes, the congregation saw the priest as an itinerant evangelist, as they were left to consult with their wardens over pastoral issues. This Church position was vulnerable without any endowment and compounded with a poor or low Church attendance, their ability to sustain their parish share was low. Looking at the parish records of the Church and under a huge amount of stress, I was able to see that this parish had over the years been in a similar situation. Their fears have always been that they might have their Church closed. Many a time however, the Church that nursed this fear is far from being closed as the fear for closure was often a catalyst for proactive ventures that would recover the situation. It is obvious that only Churches that lose the support of the parishioners or the goodwill of the residents that can close. The people have to consistently refuse giving support over a long time because the Church of England is never too keen to close any Church. To this extent people of the communities were always encouraged to be part of fund raising and the activities of the parish Church, and as the Church played her part in all the other social organs of the local community. The breakdown of communication over the years among the different segments within any village also leads to some psycho-social problems within the fellowship and common purpose of the Church which contributes to financial strain. The ancient wisdom says: '*a house divided against itself cannot stand*'. Some Church groups are also into similar situations, yet it does appear that the people concerned may be unwilling to listen to the priest whom they see as an outsider. The problem would have been resolved if the people had spent time working together to create workable models. When things got to a head, I had no alternative than to call for help from the Diocese to resolve the financial aspect and the human angle. The parish share was reviewed and the happy people began to start as friends once again.

Diocesan Contributions

My work continued to improve, as I became a member of the Diocesan Synod, the Diocesan Rural Theology Group and Task Group and later the Synod Anglican Covenant Review Group. In 2010, it was my risk to challenge some approaches in the Anglican world at the Richmond Deanery Synod during election hustling for all the candidates standing for election to the General Synod of the Church of England with a debate between all the clergy candidates. The Anglican Covenant was yet to be voted on at the General Synod, but it is my belief that a change of approach in the way of handling certain matters of the Communion is essential. In 2011, the whole question of women in the episcopacy of the Church of England came before the Richmond Deanery Synod and later the Diocesan Synod having been referred to it by the General Synod. From my first day in ministry I had always been firmly supportive of women priests and bishops in the Church. The systems of selecting Synod delegates in the Churches of England and of Nigeria are different. In the Church of England, every priest belongs to the Deanery synod and every parish in the deanery can send delegates to the Deanery Synod depending on the number of people on their electoral register. The election into the Diocesan Synod takes place from the deanery Synod, while elections into the General Synod take place from among the members of the deanery Synod and from the Diocesan Synod. The three houses of the Bishops, Clergy and the Laity elect their chairpersons and they maintain a collective presidency; however the leadership role of the Bishops is not ignored. However, in the Church of Nigeria, all priests and deacons are automatic members both of the district and the diocesan Synods. The deanery synod will be equivalent to the district Church council within the Church of Nigeria. In fact, the diocesan Synod is often referred to as the clergy annual festival, depicted by their ceremonial procession to joyful hymns at the Synod's opening Eucharist service and on the day of the official closing Thanksgiving service when different Archdeaconries would strive to outperform each other with dancing, donations and drama. There does not appear to be any tangible difference in the deanery Synods for the two Churches except that the financial position for each church and possible suggestions for Church growth seem to be the focus at such meetings. It is advantageous as each priest will prepare very well for this meeting by seeing that the demands expected from his Church has been met before venturing to attend meetings. Attendance is always required. The Diocesan Synod in the diocese of Ripon and Leeds and in the Church of England is always smoothly running. I have always loved attending these meetings because it is a family affair, with everyone respectful of others. The clergy, the laity and other bishops not presiding normally sit freely and contribute to discussions. The meetings however take place only on Saturday mornings in different locations four times in the year. In the Church of Nigeria, the Diocesan Synod is an annual celebration of ministry. The people are elected into the diocesan Synod from every church and the number of representatives depends on the financial strength of each parish. Since money plays a part in the elections of each Church, it also carries a significant part in the time and energy devoted to money matters in the Synod of many dioceses.

The Common Tenure

I arrived into the Church of England during the discussions for transition from freehold into Common Tenure. From the early 2011 the Common Tenure of the Church of England, applied to all clergy, removing the inequality between those priests with freehold and others. With Freehold, the church, the parsonage, and the church land or buildings, the so-called temporalities are in effect owned by the Freeholder of the benefice as long as he or she is in position. In England, the clergy have no contract, and are not in a legal sense 'employed'; whereas the licenced clergy under Common Tenure are in law 'office-holders'. The reality from freehold to Common Tenure is mainly to satisfy the European parliament on issues of employment rights across the board—this to a large extent seems beneficial to the welfare of the clergy. Common Tenure gives bishops more control over the clergy, and gives the clergy new rights including: the entitlement to a written statement outlining the terms of their appointment; one full day off a week; 36 days' annual leave; and access to a grievance procedure. Priests-in-charge will now be given the right to object to the Church Commissioners in the event of a proposed sale. Other rights include a minimum stipend, a right to appeal for unfair dismissal, and the right to appeal to an Employment Tribunal. Common Tenure brings with it new obligations such as the requirement to participate in ministerial development review and continuing ministerial training, and to undertake a medical examination if one's physical or mental health is suspect.

The Schools

As part of my schedule as priest in charge of the joint Benefices I was responsible for conducting collective worship in two of the schools, being Church of England aided and another being church of England controlled and to take an active role in giving spiritual direction to the affairs of the school in that capacity. The third school is a County school, but being part of one of the parishes, this places some demand on my time. It is important that when a school is in the parish, though it may be privately owned or by the Government, the students or pupils are members of the community and the priest must look after them. I as a parish priest am inclined to minister to their needs if I am allowed access, and in this County school, they are happy to receive my ministration and with much enthusiasm. However, one day I was on a training programme which was quite interesting in a positive way and the word interesting would carry the same meaning as 'amazing'. The programme was on safeguarding of children and we were reminded that it remained a taboo, and something still seen as criminal for teachers and adults among other things to touch children. It is part of the culture of protecting children in England not to touch children and this is seen as an abuse. In Britain, some touching is seen as inappropriate and steps are taken if any adult touches a youngster. Yes, some cases have already been decided by the courts involving adults who abused the children in the past. I thought to myself where is the place of genuine affection for one another? How do we show a youngster that we care, yet avoid prosecution? Are we not pushing the youngsters into the hands of abusers when those with genuine affection refrain from showing it? Yes, this is England; the law and regulations is not a respecter of persons. I am careful when discussing with anyone, as Africans are emotional people, and some mannerisms have to be stopped because it can lead to serious sanctions. Christianity as a religion is often reflected in relationships. It is also connected with ethics, morality and education generally. Children are generally sincere and honest individuals with an urge to learn more about the world in which they live, but these attributes seem to be discouraged more in our world today by using the antics of a few criminally minded adults to determine the relationships between adults and children. If a disturbed child came to class, a honest teacher would like to reassure this child without any intention whatsoever to abuse this child, but the teacher might be too careful. This may not be helpful to the child involved. Now let us imagine that a predator warmed up to such a child and the child felt that such guy is a nice one, there will be problems. This is a problem that can be solved if the teachers are not coerced into treating the child as another statistic or a missed opportunity. The child perhaps should be encouraged to grow up in a loving world but be taught how to use their mind or intuition and to report contacts at home. The child must be encouraged to grow and live in the real world, and not be quarantined from childhood to believe only in the safety of the home but learn to live appropriately and to refer issues to parents and significant others for clarification. The child though young, but from my experience in the schools I affirm that many of the children are intelligent and bold. The experience of taking devotions in schools shows me how often the children ask questions that may be adjudged to be superior to their age, understanding and experience. I was dumbfounded initially at the level of Church attendance, which as a per cent of residential population is above average; my observation is that many of the people know their God and the School children especially. The collective worship is always a spiritual trip in all the three schools within the two benefices, and many of the school children know their God and his Christ. Their questions were always very penetrating and a genuine quest to know more. Whether they and their parents rarely attend the Church or not, I had every reason to thank God for the christian presence in the three primary Schools in the communities.

In The Cathedral Of The Dales

We were met on the 1st of May 2009 by two church representatives of Holy Trinity Church, Startforth—who after the formalities at the door of the bungalow handed the keys to us. It was a very memorable day; with many cards sent to us from many of the congregations that made up the seven churches of the two benefices. On arrival in Teesdale that morning, I was not naïve enough to expect a hero's reception where everyone would receive us with open arms; as I left London with some trepidation and anxiety as to what the future would bring. It was obvious from the beginning that I had the support of the Diocese of Ripon and Leeds and the Church of England with the Parochial Church Councils (PCCs) right behind me. The Startforth church representatives assisted and ensured that I got all the help and connections that I needed to settle down properly, helping to see if the telephone worked, and the living room beautifully adorned with the flowers they gave us. Fifteen days into our stay in Startforth and four days before my installation, a representative who was in charge of the church catering organised with the members a supper to welcome us into Startforth and many of the congregation were invited. It was a wonderful evening. It gave us the privilege of seeing many people, but it was a struggle trying to remember so many names all at once. There and then I was introduced to another phase of Teesdale, the flower arrangements, which was one of the fund raising activities within the benefice. I always knew that the English have a time and sense for detail, but when the flowers were arranged I could only notice that with some willingness, the human race could add beauty to God's creation around us. That night this point could not be better proven.

The Licensing and Installation Service

My licensing and installation service at St Romald's Church, Romaldkirk was an occasion well attended, with my arrival in the area something of a novelty to the region, and reported in local and regional press—in the Teesdale Mercury, The English Churchman, Darlington and Stockton Times and The Northern Echo, with one of them in a subsequent write-up describing my appointment as a breath of fresh air and that my presence in Teesdale was already exciting a massive positive difference. The Newspapers were very generous in dedicating space of their newspapers to our arrival and publishing our pictures and interviews at every turn. One of my duties which took off from that service was to take personal responsibility for the pastoral care of the Teesdale villages that were bordered in the north by the diocese of Durham and in the west by the diocese of Carlisle in the Cumbria region of North West England. In most places, I noticed that the people appreciated a sense of prayer, care and compassion and exhibited the fundamental faith in their God and our Lord Jesus Christ. Wednesday 20th May 2009 was installation day, all seemed ready for the event. The clergy and readers robed in the Village Hall and the service started with the procession of the clergy, readers and Bishop. This was an occasion in which everyone, Christians and the village communities, business concerns along with the farming folks were all present to show their commitment to the ministry of the Church and to give their promise to support Stephen. I was grateful for all the resources committed to this by the wardens in their planning. St. Romald's was filled up that day, and in her splendour as 'the cathedral of the Dales' as she is known to be. Everyone listened to Bishop John Packer who gave the address to enrich our spirit and talk about the learning process that was about to begin, with Stephen learning from the good people of Teesdale and the parishes also sipping something from what Stephen has brought from all his experiences from Serbia, Croatia and from Nigeria. He enjoined us also to share our faith in Christ with others. The service was then followed by supper at the village Hall, where all had something to drink, eat and where fellowship was shared. Nearly everyone brought something to the table, and at the end of the reception, everyone had enough, and the leftovers were enough encouragement for another invitation to supper. Such was the generosity of the parish and of Teesdale people that it did not take long for my learning process to unfold. The reception was assisted by the cool weather condition of the spring evening, which helped in great measure the enthusiasm and warmth during the supper that lasted till late in the evening. Jeff and Carol made provision for trips to and from Darlington train station to bring our guests home. Our guests, who came up were from all walks of life and were all made comfortable by the steering committee put in place by the parishes to welcome and accommodate our guests. They included my friends from London and Nigeria, such as the Sir & Lady Osoba, Dapo & Toyin Sotonwa, Neil, Roy, Seun, Adeolu & Kehinde, Adeolas among others. My appointment was the beginning of a learning curve that seemed to be unending. I am a Nigerian by birth and to many who understand this, it may include enduring certain things that have become issues of the past century in many other countries. I would appreciate to dwell on these from a psychological and spiritual point of view. Two days earlier the rehearsal had been conducted by Rev. Stanley Haworth and everyone was aware of what was to happen in the service. There should be no surprises during the service, due to the fact the English neither expect nor like surprises. Firstly,—the symbols used for the resonation, the Fleece, walking boots, hay, Bible, Chalice and paten were to remind me of the ministry I would be having among the large rural sheep farming countryside in Teesdale. Secondly,—The Service time of 7:30pm which was strange to me since I was used to church services from 10:00am or 10:30am, however, I have since realised that most meetings if it is to be well attended in Teesdale were late in the evening. This was partly because farmers will not relax or take their attention off their flock or herd until the flock have gone to sleep, or milking is complete. Thirdly,—During the time for notices I was so carried away with emotion that the African in me came to the fore, thanking people individually and appreciating them one after the other, and that prolonged the service a bit. This error ensured that it was never repeated as I saw the need to keep to service pattern and be conscious of time. Fourthly, what happened above exposed my thick sub-Saharan accent and the pronunciations which have become part of me over the years. Trust the English to reach you with their comments when something was not exactly what they expected, some people might even feign deafness if the pronunciation was not right for them. Often there were incidents which were symbolic of other issues that could rightly be described as the tip of an ice-berg? The first in the series happened on the day of my licensing at the supper that followed the installation service. The supper took place in the village hall in Romaldkirk. I was in the crowd mixing freely with the people, sharing banter, goodwill and jokes. At one point one of the prominent persons from one of the communities came up to me, smiling and expressed what an amazing service we had just had and my rector from London asked his impression of me coming to their two benefices. This person looked at me and smiled and then facing him expressed regret that I was the one appointed for them. Having passed such a negative comment about me in my presence, I wondered what others thought about me, a deaf man or a man who could not understand any spoken English perhaps. I acted as if I did not hear this comment and I smiled. This person looked at me again and smiled and continued chatting with me as good friends do. This aspect of culture shock in which a smiling face would not typify acceptance or with a comment such as, "yes Stephen this is good" taught me to watch out for the 'red flag'. However, I must confess that this person later represented to me significant progress and positive communal contributions, as he dedicated not only his time, energy and resources; he also encouraged his family and friends to make us feel welcome. He most definitely must be thinking of something else beyond me to have made the comment that I regarded as patronising. My installation service also helped clarify my sense of family. What is family if it cannot be experienced? In my younger years, up until when I left my parents' home, my experience of growing-up within the family was very difficult. There was a lot of suffering from some members who were meant to support me, though poverty and ignorance played its part. The Thursday after my installation was the celebration of the ascension of our Lord Jesus Christ, after His resurrection from the dead. This time it was celebrated at the ruins of an ancient Abbey at Easby in Richmondshire. This open air service attracted eighty people within the deanery whose aim was to relive the experience the disciples had on the day Jesus went up back to the Father in heavens. The attendance underlined the passion and commitment of the Christians of the deanery to worship and witness the risen Christ in the ruins of Easby Abbey. The regional newspaper was awash the following day, with the proceedings of the day and with my pictures and an interview. This was only the beginning as I have been subsequently accorded the privilege of being granted interviews and having my picture adorning both inside and front pages of some newspapers. I later got an invitation from Radio Teesdale for a live interview. That was my first time of visiting a radio station and it was a learning experience also. I was a sight to behold and my anxiety must have been written all over me during my time in the studio, but Ruth the programme presenter was immensely gentle with me. It was therefore with a sense of exploring another form of ministry in my new appointment that Buki and I travelled to Teesdale, but with a daunting expectation from the churches and villages. Yes, with all my psychological and spiritual experience and preparation it was with a sense of trepidation, excitement and respect that I started my first day in Teesdale. It was all different, and the approaches to doing things culturally is different from London, or to anywhere I have ever lived and more so different from village to village within Teesdale.

Chapter Six

The Business of God's Mission

Many societies have different approaches to different issues; and this could not be more pronounced than in the area of Fund raising within Teesdale. At present, Fund raising has been elevated to a career route in many societies and of which the European societies are in the forefront. In the sub-Saharan African churches most especially in Nigeria I have reached the realisation that we did a lot of fund raising in the churches which was not so labelled accordingly. I could now, with a sense of hindsight, realise that the manner in which we collected tithes, thanksgiving offering, Harvest, Easter, Christmas and New Year offering and thanksgiving were fund raising events. Another major Fund raiser in the Nigerian Churches were the Family Harvest festivals, as each family came forward for thanksgiving annually as a means of making the families gather together and share fellowship at least once a year but with a major aim to raise money for the church. The Church societies and groups celebrate a form of patronal or founders day with the sole aim to raise awareness about their aims and objectives, and as a Church fund raising event. These raked in more than 35 per cent of the annual income for most parochial church accounts. Yet, it is only when these sub-Saharan churches formally send invitations to persons to come and donate money on a specific event that they were labelled fund raising events. At a formal Fund raising event, either in the church hall or auditorium, invitees would be encouraged to give their contributions or announcements made as the pre-set target would determine if the event is successful or otherwise. I will not like to comment on the advantages of either, but what the African Churches were doing are appropriate and helpful for them to maintain their churches if they did not want to go cap in hand begging for donations abroad. The giving also helped individuals in a way to trust God for church growth, as communities increase their congregations and build facilities. However, others who would sparingly give but rely on what others do would not hesitate to complain about paucity of their church funds while they give their money to other deserving charities. I believe that beautiful English saying which says *'charity begins at home'* implying that congregations would better serve their cause to give to Church Funds, rather than be complaining within the church while giving money to other causes. While I was in the Churches of Eastern and Central Europe, Fund raising could be in the form of breakfast, lunch or dinner, but normally involved writing a brief of the Church financial situation and seeking assistance from those who were seen to be charitable either as individuals or organisations. However, in Teesdale the methods were typical of Western Europe and the people without fanfare and in their typically quiet ways contribute their drops of water which eventually flow as a river. My first challenges were the twin invitations from Romaldkirk and Mickleton to open their Village Fair for 2009, more so because I had never done this before. At Mickleton, I was to judge fashion and beauty contest. How did I get involved with that when I do not appear to have a sense of fashion myself? I had no idea what this entailed, but I was supported and guided by the organisers as to what to do. I was eventually able, in consultation, to agree to who went home with a prize. It is not 'the winner takes all', this is an annual fair organised by the village community to foster social cohesion and contribute to various charities around. Whereas the Romaldkirk Fair invitation was for the Annual Fund-raising event for the parish of Romaldkirk with Cotherstone, with the Rector of the parish traditionally in charge, but with every parishioner doing their best in supporting the Church with the event. Within the parishes, events such as the annual Romaldkirk Fair are actively supported by the local communities, and it serves not just as a Fund raiser to the organising communities but also as a rallying point and an engine of social mobilisation and cohesion among the different families who came from different directions to settle in the particular village. At Romaldkirk for example events of the Fair often witness the presence of donkeys and it was at Romaldkirk that I came close to the donkey for the first time and the golden opportunity made possible by a lady called Dorothy to touch a horse, while the Phillip's family ensured that I rode one of their own. It was a huge kindness which was celebrated by all involved and I guessed that the horses were happy with those encounters also. Also on display at the Fair were Tombola and Raffle ticket stands along with the books, plants, coconut shy, whisky draw, white elephant, smashing china, teas and refreshments, ice cream, children's' games, cake stall, tug-o-war and the Stanhope silver band all provided entertainment for the day. When the planning committee briefed me about the events for the day and mentioned that we would be having a white elephant stand, I naturally became curious and I informed them that I have never seen an elephant which was white before, but Su my relentless administrative assistant chipped in and educated me. The white elephant stall consisted of those good items in the house which were no longer needed by the family and were donated to the church for generating funds. The smashing china event was a bit controversial, it involved wooden balls and a series of china wares placed on a stand. The aim was to hit and smash some of them after a donation, it was purely fun, but it is a helpful fundraiser. In the first year it brought in good funds into the church kitty but the do-gooders subsequently felt it was good to give away the china wares at some price to those who needed it. I thought there were good points in the arguments for both parties as both still brought in money into the Church funds. The Tug of war attracted adults and children as teams pitched their strength against one another. I joined a group which lost out as they pulled us for a distance. It was fun and it was amazingly funny when I saw my picture in the local newspaper the following day showing me smiling and pulling. I knew the editor was simply being courteous and charitable with me and because they did not publish the pictures when I was flat on my back. Sometimes there are a few summer concerts in the neighboring churches with drinks served by the local pub and the profits shared. The Churches are grateful for all the support from the communities. Even the people who do not associate with the Church are willing to give to all the charities who they believe make a difference in our world. Looking at my itinerary

Romaldkirk Fair clashed with a wedding already booked at St. Mary's, Brignall and because the latter date was in the diary handed on to me on my resumption, I quickly informed the Fair chairman of my inability to attend promptly. I was to arrive seventeen minutes late, after concluding the wedding, but as it turned out, lateness under any guise was seen by the English as a sign of disrespect to an event, even though I was humoured by some who smiled and reassured me of their understanding. I sensed that this was simply to give me a soft landing. Next at the Startforth School Fair this actually was novel to me as all sorts of ensembles were on the tables and I wondered at this point who was better amused, me or the pupils? My experience as a middle aged man, whose duty was to judge the items on the tables, which were brought in by individual pupils, is still something that amuses me till today. This made me examine how much fun I must have missed during my childhood. During my childhood, it was unacceptable to draw, to paint or even play games such as table-tennis or football. My parents believed that only rascals play games, but good children read their books or help their parents in whatever they did. How times change, and there were changes from time to time. Therefore, because I could not in any honesty rely on my ability to judge art works, I got a teacher to look at the works of art with me, and I hoped we did some justice together. The Bowes Fair was in not many ways different to that of Mickleton in organisation and purpose, but there was something unique about Bowes village. It has an old Castle ruin and it also retained the legendary old style Harvest Bazaar, with a professional auctioneer in tow. The Bowes Harvest Fruit auction sale was a wonder to behold. It reminded me of the Harvest Bazaars in Nigeria of the 1960s and 70s and I still believed, rightly or wrongly, that the foods sold at auctions were the most delicious. I thought this idea came to me in 1964 when I was only seven years old, and when I made my younger brother Adesoji share a gift of a well-prepared bean cake at the Juvenile Harvest Bazaar of St. Mary's church at Ijebu-Imusin, Nigeria. The Bowes Church Harvest Bazaar in the Ancient Unicorn Pub was filled with villagers and farmers with their families contributing happily to church funds, and as I understand it, they have been contributing to Church Funds annually over the years. The

Cotherstone Fun Weekend follows similar pattern of Bowes and Mickleton, with different age-grade fashion parades and drumming, which helped the community integration and unity. However, Cotherstone Fair has an annual side attraction which is unique to the village and which shows how ingenious, inventive and large hearted the people are. They make scarecrows which stand in front gardens, peep through bushes and hang from trees and windows during the Fun weekend. This is an evidence of how happy and positive thinking the people must be to have that great sense of creativity and humour. The event which annually is held the third weekend in the month of June involved both the young, the adults and the elderly, with a Scarecrow Trail; a Fun Run; Maypole dancing; All Fancy Dress competition; and with stalls for: Bunting, Ice cream, Balloon man, Phoenix cards, Bric a brac, Jewellery, Cake, Duck race and Tombola among others. At the Sunday of that weekend the church groups in the village that consisted of the Methodists, Quakers and the Church of England gathered on the Village Green for an ecumenical Thanksgiving service to God with the Middleton Band in attendance. If the weather was bad, the village hall would be the venue for the service. Refreshments were normally served, free of charge, after the Sunday service. It is important to note that there is a high degree of ecumenism within this area as it is usual for both Methodists and Anglicans to worship together and do things in common which served as a standard for many other villages. There are no formal meetings of a Christian association or in the form of Churches Together, yet the arrangements work perfectly well as the people see each other as members of the same community and this is excellent. At the beginning of my third year, I had a unique experience at the Bowes Church Barbeque. There was enough for everyone to eat and drink, with opportunities for fellowship and a Raffle draw. Many brought different items as donated items to be won from the Raffle draw. At a point, it was time for dancing, Christine the wife of Gilbert pulled me up to the dancing floor, and to minimise the impact of my poor dancing skills, I made known my state of dancing tactics. However, I did not need to be afraid as there were many others who dared not stand to dance whereas I did manage some hops, steps and dancing. I must have made much jokes about my dancing skills than others were ready to acknowledge. It was a novel opportunity for me to try some English dance steps. The wardens and volunteers were wonderful as the people of Bowes have often surprised me with their co-operation, especially the Bowes Women Institute. My observation across the two benefices and the people however led me to some observations. That the rural people of the north east which may typify the heartland of England are a patient people, they do not pass comments in a hurry. It took some time for some people to warm up to me, and about a year for some people to discuss more fully, but they were more global in their attitude and view of the world. There were three main categories within the rural population, and they were the farmers and farming community on one side and those who have chosen to settle into the villages on their retirement while the third category were people of other vocations. The level of a caring attitude and knowledge that are absent in the big cities were present in abundance in Teesdale, as many people who live in London and other big cities may not know what is happening in the neighbouring borough. Can we then say that there are more cosmopolitan people in the heartlands and more local people in the cities? However, I also notice that there is Christian blood running in the veins of the people, and even when they are not habitually in Church and they present deep Christian attitudes. Their children during the school assembly collective worship exhibit a deep belief and yearning for the Gospel, which they must have imbibed either at school or home or both. I must also confess that the wardens within the joining benefices possess Christian commitment and love for the Church of God, and many of the people are wonderful to be with. They are people from whom much encouragement is obtained, as they gently prod me into forging ahead with the business of God's mission in Teesdale. One morning, barely two months into my ministry I got a call from a lady who wanted to meet with me. On her arrival she spoke frankly. Her point simply was that, some people found it difficult to understand me, and she encouraged me to do something about it. This singular act of this person sealed our friendship, as I know her to be a reliable friend who can tell me the truth despite any odds. However as at that time, I was sometimes lost as to what some of the people were saying because of their accent. Therefore the learning curves seemed to be mutual. I decided to seek help and got someone who taught me public speaking, voice coaching, cultural ethos and knowing when someone was hurt, angry or just being cheeky. Some aspects of the local culture have to be known and in other words, I was determined to broaden and sharpen my communication skills and voice coaching. After sometime I began to look inwards, joked less and introversion was becoming the norm. I was also becoming tensed up and stressed to the extent that I was having a problem hearing my own voice. This to me raised a red flag and a challenge. To my admirers, I have a musical accent and they tried their best to support my ministry among them. They were my heroes in ministry for all their encouragement and support, for they kept me going. If I was feeling frustrated at one end of the benefices, the other end was helping me to stand firm and get better prepared to do my job. Yes, some people were angels and they did not realise that if I was to get any award for being in Teesdale, all the credit would go to those groups for recognising my potentials and worth. If I was selected for this job despite my accent I must not allow anything to scupper my chances of success. The act of the re-introduction of Christianity into Nigeria by the missionaries in 1842 came after the initial short-lived mission that ended in disaster due to a perceived arrogance of the missionaries who disrespected the African culture. This new introduction through Badagry port in the south west of Nigeria, which geographically locates in modern day Lagos State was a success. They came with the traders and colonialists, they spoke neither Yoruba language, nor any of the native tongues nor did the people they intended to convert speak any English. Yet today not only does the Christianity they brought thrive and flourish the English language became the lingua franca of Nigeria and many other sub-Sahara African countries. Therefore I could not see an impediment in the accent of ministering the Gospel in Teesdale, even though I agreed that there were challenges to overcome. My African accent might be an initial surprise but it would eventually be an asset, because it will remain a little different in a musical way. More so as there were all sorts of accents around here in Britain, even within the English country, there are the local London accent, the

Yorkshire, and local dialects across the counties. I weighed my options from voice coaching to elocution lessons after all I am in Teesdale for mission and I must effectively interact with the people.

An Unusual Experience

As I was grappling within myself as to the wisdom of my coming up to Teesdale, I experienced two encounters. They both occurred over a funeral. The first occurred when I was called out for a funeral service at a crematorium, and as I was greeting the relatives of the deceased who were filing out of the Chapel, one elderly male relative refused to shake hands with me and all of this particular man's children copied him. I felt disturbed, not with rage, but sadness, for I had never before experienced anything like this in my life, not even in the remote areas of Eastern Europe. This was actually happening in a big town not in the rural area and I was wondering, what could have happened in the past to the man in question that made him react in such a manner, and his children like him. As far I am concerned, all I needed was a chance meeting with the man again; perhaps there might be a pastoral opportunity there. I quickly tried to ignore the incident as if nothing has happened as I have a duty to perform and since there were others on the queue waiting to be greeted and for me to encourage and comfort them.

The Road I once Walked

Two days later, I received a call that someone died suddenly in a remote corner of a benefice. The winter of 2009 was part of our welcome package to Teesdale, as much of eight inches of snow was the average of snow fall on the ground most of the time, as temperatures remained for most part below freezing. But the winter of 2010 was nowhere comparable to the past fifty years in the U.K and America as the Arctic weather blew from the north into the United Kingdom and most of England and especially northern England was covered with a blanket of snow. The disruption caused by this unexpected weather was so horrendous that traffic and the communities stood still for days and weeks as most people were snowed in, not being able to clear their drive ways. The weather was abnormally cold even to the people who were used to the coldest winters in England. The caller was gracious enough to inform me that though the man who died had no association with the Church of England, but it was appropriate for me to give my condolences and to support the family. The man, to ensure I did not miss the directions drove ahead of me and pointed to the deceased person's home where I was to meet the dead man's wife and her sister. I managed to park close to the farm gate and walked up to the house. The ladies were in the living room and I knocked on the front door and they looked at my face, the widow decided I was not to be allowed entry. She shouted at me through the window to get away from her house and their property. However, never the type to give up without a chance, I stopped a bit longer; perhaps I could be given the chance to explain my intrusion. My perseverance was rewarded within a ten minute wait beside the road on that chilly day when a car drove up into the back of the farm house. I followed the car and the pair got out and discharged their cargo of food stuffs and drinks into the house. I explained my purpose for being there and one of the pair asked me to follow her into the house as she called the women, who by this time had gone upstairs. She climbed upstairs announcing that I am a vicar, because I was wearing a white collar around my neck. The woman popped her face down the steps and shouted she did not want to see me and that I should go away. I felt sad. Before I departed the house, I prayed for the family with the two people at the door. In an instant I remembered the famous, but martyred author Dietrich Bonheoffer, who wrote *"when God calls you, He calls you to come and die."* I asked myself if many British or Portuguese missionaries have died or been killed for the sake of their mission in many countries of the world, then I could not now go back home because of a few perceived insults and that I should stop asking if home is not far away. But for now I must get on with the mission of Christ. When I got into my car, I asked myself on what authority was I judging this woman or the previous man who refused to shake hands with me? What was my audacity for believing I knew what was going on in their minds? These people who have just lost their loved ones might be in my shoes some eleven years ago, when I was so angry with God for taking away my mother who died at the age of eighty-three years. The two dead persons died a lot younger than my parents. For many days and weeks after the funeral, I was angry with God. I asked God why he did not spare my mother's life and cure her from the massive stroke which she suffered for months. Why did other mothers go on living for ninety or a hundred years? Why did I have to suffer the death of my father and mother so prematurely? My anger stemmed from the fact that my father died before I had even completed my first month in my first Church as a priest, and could not worship with me as he fell sick shortly after I began in the Church. This was a father whose prayer life was to see me as a cleric and he did his best to support my life. He and my mother sacrificed all they could offer to see me educated. On the other hand I compensated myself by thinking that without my doting and loving father, I could be best friends with my mother, but before I could enjoy a mother from whom I have been separated to be away in Europe for so long, she had stroke and died in October 2000. I had always believed that these two sets of people needed me more than those who sat down with me for tea and cakes. Whatever made me think of perceived ridicule clearly calls for repentance on my part, *for I am not called to be served but to serve*. I did not assume it will be easy living in the part of the country where, even from the PCC Statement before my appointment, it was stated that the ethnic minority was less than 0.50%. In reality, I believe it is far less than that, because apart from Buki and I, in the two Benefices, I am able to notice only three or four other persons who appear to have had a parent from outside the EU, but they were in all probability English children. Some few days after those two incidents I was confronted with another challenging situation. In one of the churches, the warden told me a week after my arrival that she had retired before my arrival and were only waiting to step down. However she promised to do all she can in a more personal capacity. The evolvement of the economy of understanding and the law of necessity made me to allow her to be sworn in some months later. On a chilly January morning, after the Sunday service she resigned the office. Why? She definitely told me to swear her in as the warden as she felt I needed all the support and at that time there were not many volunteers in the parish. Therefore this lady in whose vein flowed kindness and commitment decided to shoulder the task as far as she could. The lady's ministry in the church is a good example of Christian commitment and faithful service. Knowing that I am naturally an extrovert and one always given to public discourse emotionally, I knew I had to make some personal sacrifices. These are part of the coping skills typical of any person in a new environment, so I examined some of the things that will make my learning smoother. I reminded myself that before I can foist opinions that I need to first learn and humbly adapt to situations and understand the culture of my hosts. I gradually metamorphose from the extrovert into introvert. There were numerous things to learn, assumptions to be discarded and opinions to be moderated if I am to achieve anything with my ministry in Teesdale such as

a) noting that a bride could arrive late for her wedding.

b) People might just turn up at the door without any prior appointment.

c) People indicating they were hard of hearing, sometimes refusal to comment on an issue might mean you were saying something offensive, and not politically correct.

d) That people have said "OK", "This was good" and "smile" at you might not be a sign of approval. You might need to wait for some time after a meeting, to confirm your agreement before action is taken. This obviously explained why in the western way of doing things, there is always provision for the Minutes of the last meeting to be taken, agreed upon and approved, before being signed by the chairperson.

e) It is also significant to be aware of body language. Any change of attention, facial colour or posturing might be an important factor deciding when to stop or postpone discussions on an issue.

f) That I can be rung up as early as 8.00am in the morning or as late as 11.00pm in the night by someone seeking an appointment or wanting to know if the parish magazine is ready and why she/he has not received her copy. It does not matter if I had seen a copy or not.

g) The death of anyone at whatever age demands respect and sensitivity is expected for handling it from all concerned. For funerals the attendees would have been seated as much as 20-30 minutes before the service. The partying and the dancing, celebrations or Fund raising associated with other provinces during a funeral service have no place in the English Church. More-so, a charge is made for the service in the Church of England, and further donations are given at the discretion of both the family and those who attend.

For whatever reason, it gradually began to dawn on me that a shock be it an electric shock or a culture shock, could leave an individual with the same devastating effect. In comparison to all the other places I have ever lived Teesdale is a serene, quiet and peaceful place. I had enjoyed my fair share of noise, and noisy social activities in many places in the past and a good public transport system in the cities, but Teesdale is a place where some activities cannot be taken for granted. I recollect the feedback I received from two members of a parochial church council (PCC) when after a PCC meeting in one of the parishes I introduced the idea of having praise worship and choruses during services. They threatened to withdraw their participation in Church if that is to happen. I was keen to introduce this, but without the chaos of having some of the congregations pulling away. The mid-point view was consolidating the newly formed House Fellowships and Prayer meetings. At other times, I had learned to play deaf, instead of reacting to every single thing that annoys and sometimes there have been times when I had pretended to be ignorant, or unable to understand, the direction of a discussion which I know may lead to irritation or potentially sensitive feelings. After some months trying to understand the accents and overcoming other cultural barriers and with June Armstrong trying her best to assist me with voice coaching and building my communication skills, I began to adapt to life in county Durham. I would be honest enough to confess that on my arrival the sheer weight of all these afore-mentioned issues gave me initial stress, so much that I felt as if I was walking through a maze. Sometimes I would visit a church or community and it seemed to me as if I was passing through whatever happened there as a man blind folded. After twelve months I was becoming more hopeful than ever before and I was beginning to notice that I was gaining more friends within the Church and the community. I was beginning to notice land marks which have been in existence tens or hundreds of years before I arrived the communities. I shall also say that I had a profound sense of isolation at certain points in my ministry, even though this is the lot of many priests and ministers across the world. For about sixteen months of my being installed, the nearest rector to me in the Diocese of Ripon and Leeds was in Aldbrough St John and that was about thirty eight miles return journey from my residence. I should explain that the diameter of my benefice and return journey is thirty miles from the eastern edge to the western edge. I could email and telephone, but it is not a good substitute for personal communications when the need for fellowship arose. Perhaps I can summarise the contributions of some people who like pillars of enterprise, had specific impact on my ministry in Teesdale. The wardens and parish secretaries were simply fabulous and amazing in charm and commitments and every member of the PCC were trying their best to contribute to growth. Even in the isolated cases where there were differences of opinion the intentions of the individuals could not be faulted. It was a divinely appointed arrangement across the different parishes with the ways things run smoothly, and in no time I was surprised to note how fast the time flew past. I had attempted listing the personalities before I realised how very difficult it turned to be as there are different models to choose from within the benefice. Let us take for example: Ms Aye is a secretary of a PCC, an energetic person and committed, and a person for whom I have huge respect. I will want to write a book about this person, but for now I have decided to write only on issues with limited contributions to my ministry in Teesdale hence I shall constrain myself to this aspect. Though at times she might have said things that seemed to unnerve me, I am sure she meant well. She tried her best always as a bridge builder and liaise with us as one who has wider exposure of life herself. She appeared to me to have attained comfort for her family by virtue of hard work, and her common sense is always able to assist the Church. She is a marvellous character blessed with a wonderful family. For about two years, I was privileged to have Bp. David, an assistant Bishop in our diocese who was residing in one of the parishes assisting with some of the services, and he was a willing and helpful bishop. In the Church of England as a priest or bishop, it is not permitted for one to retire into the parish, benefice or diocese where you have just retired from, and Bp. David on his retirement as the neighbouring Diocesan has retired into a house in the benefice, taking up the position of an assistant Bishop in the Diocese. Rev. Pete, typified the retired priests and readers who shared the ministry with me within the benefice and our relationship is very helpful from the very beginning of our ministry in Teesdale. He is selfless and committed to evangelism, always willing to assist in any way possible, and an asset to us in terms of human resource, he typifies the assistant clergy and readers within the benefice. I don't know how I would have survived without his help and insight. Often merely looking at him comforts me, why? This is because this man spent many years in one of the communities in this benefice and he is so experienced. Shirley, his wife made for me a special hand-woven woollen jumper for my first winter in Teesdale which remains hugely appreciated. Rev. Pete is a warm character. All the assistant or associate priests and readers were great on their tasks for the Gospel. I knew from the very beginning after my ordination into priesthood that I am an imperfect person striving to minister to an imperfect congregation with the prayer that the perfect God by His Spirit shall continue to teach us. The benefice is privileged to have a mix of both male and female retired clergy, among who were theologians of national and international repute serving on the bodies of the World Council of Churches. Peter, Elizabeth, Janet, Moore, Judith, Anne, Stables, John, Judy, Doug, Penny, Mary,

Colin, Sue, Ghita, Celia, Keith, Jeff, Heather, Joyce, Carol, Ian, Jennie, Frem, Isabel, Arnold, Betty, Margaret, Carl, Jim, Rosemary, Liz and David were also of massive assistance to our ministry. Gilbert, Sotonwas, Osobas, Ogunbanjo, and CJ Davies and his family of St. Nicholas, Tooting the Mitre, London, Pauline, Norman, Linda, Hazel, Freddie, Martin, Barbara, Rogers, Tom, Harry, Jillian, George, Ross, Philip, Gerald and Jennifer contributed massively to this ministry. I am grateful to be honoured by the presence of these fine Christians who with us share both the fellowship and the liturgical life of the Churches within the two benefices. Mr. Gil: He is a great communicator and I learnt to use certain words from him. He loves to describe the weather as horrendous whenever it was raining. Quite the typical British rain that is normally associated with cats and dogs! This is to me actually more like ants and butterflies compared with tropical rain in Africa that comes with actual thunderstorms. He is an articulate man, a man who could rival any ambassador of any country in the art of diplomacy. He is selfless, and always contributes his efforts and wisdom to the service of God and his community. It is definitely a great plus to have him in attendance at meetings, and if for any reason the secretary was not in attendance, here too you will get a willing and committed soul giving his best, forthright with his contributions.

Chapter Seven

Stephen in Teesdale

Teesdale is always a tourist's destination for most of the year from spring to autumn and many of the houses on the moors run bed and breakfast guest houses, and are crawling with tourists, most especially of walkers in groups, trudging up and down the bridle paths and age-old land marks. The communities which I served included the communities of Baldersdale; Boldron; Bowes; Brignall; Cotherstone; Gilmonby; Holwick; Hunderthwaite; Kelton ; Laithkrik; Lartington; Lunedale; Mickleton; Rokeby; Romaldkirk and Startforth which constituted the lower side of the river Tees which was originally part of North Yorkshire but moved to the county Durham in the local government review of 1974 in England. During the winter months the villages sometimes appeared lonely most especially in the evenings. The villages of Teesdale might not be as spectacular as their main market town of Barnard Castle which is home to GlaxoSmithKline pharmaceutical industry which is the largest employer of labour in the area, but the opportunities of the two benefices were abundant.

After A Review

Sometimes among my challenges in Teesdale I wondered if it was worth the while due to the small size of some congregations. Besides, the Church expenditure remained constant either in human or financial cost of services. The priest would still spend the same time and energy preparing a sermon either to ten or five thousand people, and the heating, water and electricity cost would still be constant while those who attend to services like putting on the boiler and preparing the church building for services and assist with readings would still offer the same service no matter the size of congregations. Yet, there is a huge sense of parochialism at work that has led to the closure of many churches in many places. The stress and frustrations were perhaps being multiplied in different parishes whereas the services can be rationalised. The fact is that there is no guarantee that people will worship in other places if their parish church was not hosting the services and that will disfranchise some believers. I will continue to be hopeful but fearful of psychological meltdown. Often the questions I asked myself is: How can I serve a people whose Christian heritage spans over a thousand years in such a way that the Gospel would become or remain challenging and yet refreshing? Secondly, should we allow people who believe in Jesus Christ to be much burdened as to become custodians of ancient Church buildings only? Was that what we were there for as Christians? Are we not as Christians meant to be evangelists of the grace of Christ Jesus? How can we then love our Jesus served in the buildings which was built to worship the Christ and the people outside for whom Christ Jesus also died? To find some answers to these questions I set out to convene a dialogue of all the PCC members of the two benefices in one place, having first got the consent of the resource persons. At the beginning of my third year after a review of the situations on ground, I invited all the parochial church councillors to a Church growth seminar which was led by James, the Bishop of Knaresborough and Paul the diocesan clergy ministerial development adviser. The positive attributes of the PCC members came out shining and there were various suggestions. I was able to gather approval for some ideas and new ones came on board. It was obvious that the period of decision has arrived and that I could not afford to shy away from taking risks for Christ Jesus. I have in the past allowed myself to be tailored because I was new to the area and I wanted to get acquainted with the structures on the ground before experimenting on new ones. But could I claim that I was so new anymore? No, I should hit the ground performing for that was why I was appointed and the expectations were high. But yes, in Teesdale no matter how long you have lived in an area you might still be a new-comer if your parents were not born in the village. One of my trusted allies in

Bowes has lived in the village for close to twenty years, has been secretary of different events over the years, but is sometimes referred to as a new-comer. However, this was not the issue of the church in the village even though no matter how much I lived I should still be cautious of native intelligence whenever the issues of the village in the church is on-going. During the seminar, the majority of the PCC members were positively inclined for the development of their benefice. That day was a day of decision and it was a happy day based on the decisions made and I confidently thanked them for things were looking good. I could say that with the level of support which I had received from the communities, I am confident of progress. As the focus of administration in the Church of England were vested in the parochial Church councils as the first contact of decision making, any agreements from the Benefice structures or district Committees still have to be ratified by each of the PCCs. However one PCC was not keen with any of the arrangements made, and they used their veto. At the PCC meeting, I listened patiently to the shooting down of the joint plans of the benefice from those who were present at the joint decision. During the meeting I constantly reminded myself, that silence was Golden in such a situation and that I am not installed to become a super hero, to achieve what others could not do but rather to sensitise the populace by my presence to the need for them to be aware of their ministry as Christians. I saw a clearer need of my role as a parson, a constant reminder to the people that God through the church remained constant in his presence and love for the communities. I decided to work on any platform available to me for success as I recollected the picture of Bp. Oluwole Olowoyo. I realised that many like me in the past have travelled all over the world and preached the Gospel, this included the British, Portuguese missionaries and in recent past the television-evangelists and mega-church founders. They preached and shared the Gospel not because the world was perfect and they did not bore us to death with their perfections either. Oluwole, the late bishop of Ijebu who ordained me said; *'when you get to a man's house and he entertains you, enjoy your visit and do not go about his house looking for cobwebs and dirt. Be positive and that is how you can ever get to his heart"*. I am also comforted by the words of Acts 6.3f " . . . . *choose seven men from among you who are known to be full of the Spirit and wisdom. We will turn this responsibility over to them and we give our attention to prayer and the ministry of the word"* The question might remain, what will happen if those entrusted with the responsibility of passing on the christian tradition and telling the story of their amazing experience of God's dealings in their family and communities should stop doing so, or hesitates to shoulder the responsibility? Will there still remain any tangible strength and time left for the ministry of the word? But the words of Paul kept ringing in my ears from 2 Corinthians 4. 18 " *So we fix our eyes not on what is seen, but on what is unseen, since what is seen is temporary, but what is unseen is eternal"* and further challenged by his instruction in 2 Timothy 4.5 when he said " *But you, keep your head in all situations, endure hardship, do the work of an evangelist, discharge all the duties of your ministry".* I had a most profound experience, yet it was a challenging situation for which there is a need for freshness to deal with the situation. I decided to develop more proactive friendship evangelism, and to chat one on one to individuals with the prayer that God is able to water what is being planted. I started the table-tennis group started to groom a Band to play my talking drums and Calabash-shakers for different occasions. I must mention my good friends Chris and Marjorie who ensured that I am never short of fresh fish. Chris would catch and prepare a lot of big fishes, bigger than the ones I had ever seen in the markets, and pack them for me. Marjorie made sure that I was never timid to collect them. Or how could I have survived if I had not got the men, boys, girls and women to play table-tennis with in Barnard Castle or in Romaldkirk, whose age ranges from 15-82 years. Dot is spectacular, she had been playing competitive games since the 1950s in London, and she still used her own rackets to play marvellous games. Yes, the villages were going to remain where they are but there is a way to move forward and organise the parishes. We trusted that the almighty and benevolent all powerful God is fully in charge of our lives. God indeed used the challenges to change me, from the person that I was, into the kind of person that I should be, a humble, sensitive and a considerate child with the joy of God constantly in my heart.

The Startforth House Garden

Even though nearly everything is in the community except my food specialities, I had a wonderful mix of parishioners, children of all ages, shopkeepers, civil servants and professionals. Some travel every day to places as far as Middlesbrough, Newcastle or Northallerton while some return from London every weekend. Apart from the vast majority who are pensioners others work on the farms and during the harvest or lambing can be out working from dawn to dusk. When I arrived Teesdale, being so completely different to the cultural setting especially in south-east London, I was faced with the question of appropriate cultural response. This was explicitly manifested first in the exchange of greetings and the manner of the exchange. I learnt later that unlike the Serb culture, male-female greetings are quite different to male-male. In my front garden was a tablet depicting how close a gardener is to nature and God, and quite a reminder to me how very present God is in our daily living and his interaction with us. In many of the villages people live as close family units, and of course many of them are related,—an offense to one might become an offense to all. Such was the level of communal cohesion and a fondness not only for their commercial animals but with their pets also. Jobey was a good fellow who would walk his dog, come rain, come snow; anything to the contrary would be seen as animal cruelty. The animals occupy a prime position in the lives of the people, and sometimes it was difficult finding out if the people were walking the dogs or the dogs were leading the way. Many dog owners and their dogs often remind me of Dogi my pet many years ago. I got him while I was on the National Youth Service Corps at Ibadan, the largest city in Nigeria and second largest city south of the Sahara desert. I got to know Dogi in an interesting situation. The landlady next door had just delivered a baby and on discharge from the hospital, everyone had gone to their home to welcome home the new child and her mother. The proud father had gone into the house to prepare a bed but found that their pet refused to get off their matrimonial bed. He tried and in desperation to get the dog to leave the place found that the dog had recently given birth to a set of puppies. The scene was hilarious and weird as the family had to deal with the mess which the newest arrivals into their family brought along with the attendant joy. The baby child had to make way for the puppies in the meantime. I looked one of the puppies in the eye and decided I should have my very first pet, and this pet gave me the opportunity of showing him love and attention in life. I was hesitant to take the puppy home as I knew that my parents never had one in the house, but the family to my surprise respected my wish and accepted Dogi into the family. In order to make it easier for the family to call the Dog by name, I simply added the letter 'i' to the word 'Dog', as the emphasis was always on the last syllable in my mother tongue. Dogi had quite an exciting but short life before he met with an accident due to human error of judgement. The memory of Dogi remained indelible, and I refused for many years to get another pet because of the fear of parting with such a wonderful fellow as my dear Dogi. In Teesdale I was introduced to a fifty years old Tortoise which is a pet of Celia. I could not imagine that I learnt a lot about the nature of a tortoise in Teesdale than I learnt in Africa even though my nickname from my secondary school days had been 'Tortie'. The tortoise I learnt would be 'laid to rest' and would fast throughout the wintry months in a cardboard box when he would sleep off till the advent of spring when he would come alive again in the warm months. However, I discovered that I have not seen such a big a tortoise in England as the African ones, which were normally huge as they grow older, and this might be the effect of the European tortoise spending half their lives fasting and sleeping. But all the pets were taken care of in a pleasant and loving way. No wonder Francis, writes St Bonaventure, called "creatures, no matter how small, by the name of 'brother' and 'sister' because he knew they had the same source of himself". Till today, within any Friary of St. Francis of Assisi, you would still be introduced to Sis. Agnes or a Sis. Joan if you did not mind that this sister or brother might be a cat. Francis thought that divine love establishes a kinship between all living things, more so as Jesus was able to be comfortable with wild animals in Mark 1.13 without any attempt to tame them, or to see them as enemies. I developed a better and far greater appreciation of nature; the moon, stars, the birds and the land in Teesdale than when I was in Africa, and because of the love of observing the birds and the cosmos I bought a telescope, and this invariably drew me closer to the appreciation of God. Some of the farmers were not finding it exactly rosy, yet they were contented with whatever they had got and many have a ministry in the parishes, as some tend the clock, sweep the chimney, led the auction, prepare the tea, set the boiler, act as sacristan amongst others. They knew what they were doing and they were respected and loved for what they do in the community. Within the Pennines of this north riding in Teesdale, I will always recognise it as a huge privilege to serve the parishes. Without the team work and the collaborative ministries of the wardens, secretaries and the PCC members, it would have been impossible for me to have stayed three months in Teesdale, and nothing would have been achieved or maintained. The Teesdale area appealed to the evangelist in me and I fell in love with the beauty of the Teesdale scenery and her people. Even though my appointment in 2009 was much of a culture shock to me as it was to many people of the region. After two years, I was still wondering what effect my being here had brought to the area. I learnt to affirm my presence, and to encourage myself that despite everything I will see to it that I am not stampeded to take any action for which history may not be sympathetic with me. I keep reminding myself that this indeed is a special school of life for me, learning what it is to persevere, be patient and humble before the Lord. I kept going back to the Bible especially, the story of Elijah when he fled before the Lord and what perhaps made such a strong prophet become intimidated to hide in caves and lamenting before the Lord. The lessons of Elijah, the caves, prophets of Baal, the earthquake, the fire and the still silent voice—that led to Hazael, Jehu and Elisha modulated my thoughts and I kept asking the Lord for strength, wisdom, courage and above all his Spirit. I began to beat my African drum, listening to praises and worship in my spare time whenever I was not practising the art of listening to God. Of course there was no hiding place for me and Buki in Teesdale, because of our distinctive features, and everyone knew Stephen and Buki on the streets, supermarket or in the church, to the extent that any other black person on the streets was seen as either Stephen or Buki or a relative who came to visit. There was an incident that happened just when we were seven months in Teesdale, when one black lady with a child was noticed in Barnard Castle. The lady had allowed her child to urinate close to the cash machine in front of a Bank in the centre of the town and this was noticed by a few people at that particular time of the morning. Just like a wild fire, rumours were rife in town as to how Stephen's young son had defiled the cash machine while his wife looked on. The following week it became hard for me to pass through the centre of the town or being in the supermarket without someone asking for an explanation on the incident. At every point I had to explain, that my youngest child was a young adult of about twenty-five years old and I was yet to have a grand-child at that time, and that I was living alone with my wife in the area. Obviously, someone whom I never knew passed by and the lady and child's attitude were passed on as mine simply because they were of African descent. In that type of community, I was always in the public eye because of my unique background and position. I also contribute to the weekly local newspaper. Two of the parishes also produced monthly and bi-monthly parish magazines and church involvements and other interviews were printed regularly in both the local and national newspapers, and of course it was never my intention to hide from anyone. Though, a section of the Church was looking for a strong, autocratic leader, I refused to be so tempted and behaved naturally, true to type as a 'band-leader' type of leader. I wanted only to be a team mate along with others in moving the Church forward, determined not to be over-forceful or arrogant to believe that I was the only person with an answer. Of course, I always have definite views as to my expectations of certain issues, and firm convictions but I am sure to contribute my opinions into a common pot of ideas along with others and then decide what was best for that time and situation. Often I go shopping twice a month at the supermarket in Barnard Castle, even though I enjoyed the luxury of shopping online for our family needs with Tesco, yet for evangelism purposes it is advantageous being at the big stores and on the streets. This is because being the biggest supermarket in the market town an evening's shopping makes more contacts with the people possible. Sometimes during the evenings, it is an opportunity to have a chance meeting with people and an occasion to ask about everything including the family, pets and the weather.

The Land Owners in the Garden

At other times, even though I am not from a family of drummers, the African talking drum is my favourite and for some psycho-social reasons, I got some African drums from Nigeria which served my purpose even by just casting a glance at them in the house as well as actually enjoying the melody that they produced. These compensatory acts helped deal with the loneliness of being the only known minority family in my area of Startforth in north-east England and reduced my stress. The vocation as a priest certainly produced its own stress no matter where one is located, but the spiritual and psychological services which Canon Leslie Morley and Neil—my spiritual directors rendered ensured that I remained human during my stay in Teesdale. Sometimes, I would wander into my back garden and behold the beautiful lives of the birds that came to enjoy my garden. Sometimes, I asked myself, who owned the garden, is it me or the other creatures like the birds, the worms and other insects that have made that place home. One day I was in the garden to show my friend Ian Nuttal a new discovery. The previous evening I saw two frogs—one golden in colour and the other blue. I have never seen that colour of Frogs in my life. I was confounded and the glory of them was amazing. God has continued in His creative acts whether we knew this or not. The other creatures in my garden perhaps have their great forebears born or nurtured in the place, and I was the first generation of my family in that house, and I was helped by the residing frogs and birds to know that the house and its environment did not fully belong to me. I am a co-occupier of the house and its gardens, and the world and all occupiers belong to God. Therefore I hated to disturb the creatures whom I considered rightful co-owners of the land, and who had no other place to call their bedrooms and dining—table except the bare garden which their progenitors had worked upon in their generations. Therefore, a mere stroll in my garden always seemed to me to be a spiritual journey of a sort that is always refreshing to my heart. My garden was a thing of novelty for me as I never contemplated having a garden where anything grows as a small farm. My existentialist way of life has always looked at an animal and seen only meat, looked at plants and seen only vegetables and not for the love for them or the beauty they radiated. I have in the past tried without success to grow yams, pepper and tomatoes hoping to make the best of the place even if I should be transporting them on a daily basis between my garage and the open gardens. Just like my front garden, the back garden is a piece of a field bordered by the concrete pads on which were the garden table with four chairs to enable us to enjoy a barbeque in the summer and two long pews under the garden shed for refreshing and relaxation. Beyond these is the perimeter wall and just before this fence in rich aluminous soil were plants and flowers of different kinds. The Ivy is conspicuous on the walls and no person in the garden can fail to notice the grand standing of the Elder tree with her subtle hollow stems from which children many years ago often produced pipes, in its maturity also producing little black berries out of which some people traditionally make wines. The Dandelions and the Digitalis also known as Foxglove beaconed from the ground with their beautiful purple flight paths. In both the front and my back garden were many Sycamore trees, a tree made popular by the legendary biblical figure—Zacheaus the tax collector who because of his height climbed one in order to see Jesus and who on meeting with Jesus hosted our Lord to a dinner. Besides the mentioned plants were the Brambles—for that is the local name for wild Blackberry which often compensates me with its delicious tokens during the warm months and beyond these were the Bluebell. Also on many parts of the wall as they climbed the fence and dotted all over much of the garden with their yellow beautiful poppies are the Welsh poppies surrounded by the Thistles, which are a relation of the Dandelions. Further down the fence are the Honey Suckle which produced a beautifully smelling aroma in the evening, and as if they are in a warm embrace with the Clematis also known as 'Old man's beard'. The Lilly, the Chives and the Geranium with their beautifully adorned blue petals in the company of two types of Hibiscus plants—the yellow and green leaved ones, the Lilac tree in company of the Prefect, Heather, Cotoneaster, the Buddleia and the Willow were another lovely group. I do behold the beauty and spectre of the Rhododendron which were typically believed to have originated from the Himalayas, but in my experience were plants that are in abundant supply on the hilly terrace of the Idanre Hills of Nigeria. But these were never appreciated by me when I was in Africa as a flower, perhaps because familiarity has been allowed to breed contempt. Besides these plants are the variegated Ivy and the Ground Elder whose roots were edible to some people in Europe. All these plants spoke volumes to me in times of stress as I looked at them often followed by my dear 'Black Bird' friend.

All Work Plus Play

Some landmark events such as the 2009 Rokeby event and the 2011 Open air Ascension day service in the ruins of the Egglestone Abbey were events that were held as Benefice events which were two of the highlights of my stay in Teesdale. These events afforded me the opportunity for the first time of exploring and, like Mungo Park while he was on river Niger, enabled me to discover the peace along the Rivers Greta and Tees and the concord of their banks. At the Rokeby event, after the exploits by the river Greta, I came out to play two games of cricket and croquet, that I have never had the opportunity to appreciate the strength which those who indulge in the game must have. I have before this day joked at the game of cricket as a child's play and then on this day I joined in the game after having first declared to those on the pitch my ignorance. After about twenty minutes in different roles I ran out of breath and felt the strength leave my legs. I agreed that truly the game of cricket is for the strong and wise. The running involved was in itself an opportunity for those gathered to make some fun out of me. I would chase the ball and run short of catching it. I chased the ball all over the pitch, it was enough to cheer the people. At first, I was ignored by the vast majority who were busy munching their snacks and chatting with each other, but as the running intensified, I became quite a spectacle to behold. The people were used to seeing me in my cassock—alb in the church decked with stole, service books and respectably bespectacled, and it was fun as I chased the ball in different directions with many miscalculations on my part. They asked me about my experience after my stint in the game, and it amused quite a lot of them to know how ignorant I was about the game of cricket, and this encounter made me realise how efficiently such games makes people relax. Some people whom I had never seen in a relaxed mood shared jokes and banter.

When The Cash Flow is Challenged

Among the parishes during the period of recession in the economy, some of the Churches were affected differently with the financial challenges. Unfortunately, some PCC members never think of the feelings of the priest when things are difficult, and they often forget that priests are also unhappy if their Churches are in financial dire straits. Some wardens or treasurers at this point will always want to show the priest that it was his entire fault, after all, year in year out the church have always remained solvent, the national economic climate affecting contributors to the church funds notwithstanding. A congregation was particularly feeling the pressure of dwindling resources that they were not happy to pay their parish share. In fact, the church believed that they have been unfairly charged. They showed me the various letters that had been written to the Diocese without any effort to reduce their share. So being in post for over a year, I requested for a meeting of the Diocesan officers with the members of the PCC to thrash out the issue. At one point during the meeting, someone made a remark that appeared to some of those present as prejudiced of me. The statement made was that some people stayed away from the church because of my presence. If a pin had dropped everyone would have heard the sound of it. I was stunned. It was clear this person meant no harm and the other PCC members refuted the insinuation and one after the other explained the circumstances of those who have not been seen in recent times. The Diocese after some further deliberations granted the church a reprieve of both what they owed as historic debt and also a reduction of their current parish share. However, I kept cool, and remembered my father's advice to 'be careful on what comes out of one's mouth whenever one is annoyed, disturbed or happy'. After the meeting, some of those present tried to reassure me as they made for their cars. I knew that nothing could be achieved if perseverance was not imbibed. This singular episode emboldened me to make the best of my stay in Teesdale. That evening, I was grateful for not driving away from the church in my car and I resisted attempts by well-wishers who wished to give me a lift, as I was desperate to have a walk, a thoughtful good walk. Taking a walk whenever I met with a challenging situation always affords me the opportunity to think things through, and it was important this should be accomplished before I returned home. I took the longer route, which was perhaps three times the distance to my favorite spot from the church, on that cold and wintry evening reviewing the situation. I looked back at the Nigerian Church and wondered if what was said could not have been said to me in the Nigerian church, where tribal prejudice was rife, and where it was common for people not to be taken as an indigene no matter how long you lived in a particular region just because your parents were not originally born into that region. I reasoned as to why people of my tribe would still look down on others because of events that must have occurred over a hundred years ago. Is the law of retribution at work here? No. I affirmed that when people behave genuinely, errors are bound to be made and we must all agree that it is normal for humans to make mistakes no matter how brutal this may appear. This person is a friend and what this person has said publicly was not unknown to me as an opinion some might have foisted on this person before then, and a suggestion I did not make attempts to correct, but I worked assiduously to rectify. With all their best intentions, my sympathisers and the diocesan officials had said their bit and left, for that was all they could do. Even though I was smiling, yet like Mary who stood weeping outside the tomb of Jesus, I closed the church iron gate and walked the distance from the Church door through the rows of tombs to the gate of the church yard, and on to the road as I began cautiously my meditations on the snow-filled deserted road on a long walk. God did not give me much time to brood over this issue as I had a meeting to attend the following week in the house of this person whom I knew as a very good helper and a friend who has stood in the gap on other issues that mattered. I was also concerned for her welfare because she seemed to be unhappy at the turn of events during the meeting, and she left after the meeting in a tense manner. As a person who had been misunderstood before in life, I was not forgetful of the good counsels I had received from this person in the past, therefore I arrived at her house earlier to chat with her. Her first shot at me when I was seated was 'Stephen, how did you feel about that meeting?' I seized the opportunity with both hands and gave her a reassurance and a lift from the valleys, and our friendship picked up again from there. I shall continue to be grateful to this friend for among other things she strenuously enabled me to acquire far more skills than would have been possible without her, as she is one of God's gifts for the sustenance of faith in the area. I know how easy it is to be embroiled in disaffection because one's feeling have been hurt, and to lose the blessings of fellowship from individuals because of the presence of imperfections manifested in the other person, or of errors committed. I am not perfect either, and I struggle towards perfections daily. This to me is not just a compromise but part of the beauty of being able to live in peace with others, by giving constant positive regard to all people, even when we recognise the mistakes committed within our relationships.

The Church Meets

The Vestry and the Annual Parochial Church Meetings (APCM) were quite lively and an education in some of the parishes but this is not replicated in some other parts. When I shared the events of a vestry meeting with my spiritual director, he simply asked me a question. How long were my immediate two predecessors in office in that particular parish? How did the people talk about them to me? How successful were social events like the Christmas fair or other annual fairs in the parish? Do they mix well with others? After I had given the answers, he kept quiet for some time and as a wise old man, he said: You cannot do anything by your power except by God's Spirit and with their cooperation. You can only do your best.' In all the places where people manifested cooperation and volunteered for different roles within the parish, there were progress and peaceful coexistence. The PCCs in many areas encouraged dialogue and people participated in discussions and were part of the worship life and were willing to be of help in any area of church and community life. This makes it easier to have prayer and house fellowships and thriving Lent courses. In one of the parishes someone who wanted to remain in the PCC only attended just a service annually and traditionally, that is the Christmas service; this made some particular people unhappy. I inherited this situation and the system was working fine for those who elected her. I did appreciate the maxim: Do not change a system that is working well'. The lady however was very helpful to my ministry. She was quite helpful to her community and to the local community school and development associations which she served dutifully. When the lady eventually stepped down, not because anything was done or said by me, it was disturbing to note how hard it was to fill the vacancy. It may be helpful if people realise that the approach of any group can be a turn off or attraction for others. Many a time vocal laity brought with them into the Church secular business approaches into the management of charity business, and sometimes were not willing to listen to any dissenting opinions. These can ease out of the Church others with dignity who might have contributed some commitment into Church life. Of course, like any organisation, the church groupings are not perfect. In fact, we must never forget that people gather into Church because of their imperfections and in prayer asking the perfect God to keep them on the path of perfection. When any individual believes that he or she should be obeyed and keeps blocking any suggestions from other individuals, there are then bound to be concerns for interpersonal relationships. I watched, prayed and gave counsel as I cautiously tried to improve my pastoral relationship with all those concerned. Therefore I decided to intensify the scriptural approach by focusing on Bible studies and prayers at every given opportunity and on Sundays. In many places in other Provinces, it would virtually be impossible for anyone to be a chorister without being present for some sessions of choir practice and be seen regularly to attend the Church. Within the benefice where there is an occasional choir, it is with joy that I encouraged the people who sang about three or four times in a year—Christmas, Easter and Harvest. No one was ever turned away, as those who came in and sang at these periods believed they were serving their community and also contributing to the festivity of the various seasons. Some of these people were professional actors and singers and it was always melodious as the choir led by the organist is an excellent contribution to worship. As priest in charge I was expected to act as the de facto vicar for each of the seven Churches, as if I had been inducted as the rector for each parish, and the parishioners saw me in that light, hence their expectations of me. They expected me to be on the ground 24/7 as their community pastor, and be present at their request any time. However, the only possible option for me was to act more as an overseer with responsibility for all and yet able to delegate responsibilities to other helpers and those with whom I shared the ministry. This meant that I was thinly on the ground everywhere. Sometimes, I saw myself as a fire fighter who dashed from place to place to maintain harmony, but at a huge cost, with a yearning to recharge my spiritual batteries in between services. This led to my fear that the ingredients essential for spiritual growth of the people may not be dispensed in a systematic way; hence I adopted an episcopal role in the multi-parish benefices.

A visit to Brampton

It is not the tradition or the culture in the Church of England for priests to hand over to each other physically. A new appointee must not be seen in any Church where he or she is appointed till during his installation service, also the incumbent that has just left office must not try to reside within the parish where he/she has just served. Because there is no location and transfer policy in the Church of England, each priest applies and is interviewed for positions as they are made available. The priest leaving a parish for another has a responsibility to resign giving adequate notice to the Bishop before taking up further appointments. Sometimes it was quite interesting listening to what parishioners have to say about one's predecessors. One of the priests that struck me as an enigma is Roy. He was like his successor—Peter, a representative of the sovereign and the rector at St Romald's more than eleven years before my advent into Teesdale, I understood that he loved horse riding within the parish. It was with joy that I went with Ruth to Brampton in Cumbria to visit Marie, the wife of Roy. Marie had sent many requests to know if I would be willing to share their generosity. It was a pleasant drive to North West England, and we listened to the stories of Roy both in Romaldkirk and after his retirement. Some of Roy's clerical wear were given to me to distribute to those who may be interested, and it was discharged with gratitude. 'The saying is true,' *that to live in the hearts of the people is never to die'.*

Looking for a Name !

In my ministry as priest in charge of the two joining benefices, it was the intention of the Church of England to have a name to call the newly forming joint benefice without having to read such a lengthy sentence such as" The joint benefice of Romaldkirk with Cotherstone and Laithkirk and Startforth with Rokeby with Boldron and Brignall and Bowes". I began the process of consultation without intending to be another Lord Luggard, the erstwhile British colonial governor who amalgamated the northern and southern protectorate around the river Niger into a country that is known as the Federal Republic of Nigeria till today. The wife of Lord Luggard, not wishing her husband to be stressed in finding a name, came forward after a thoughtful moment with a name—'Niger—Area'. Yes, and the name of the country is Nigeria !! That was how a huge land mass with about two hundred and fifty nations and tribes and languages came together to become a country with a population of about one hundred and sixty million people today. This population ensured that from every four Africans, one of them is a Nigerian. All the parishes were urging me to think of a name, and some went on to suggest it shall be called 'Stephen's benefice', but I knew that will be a proposition neither helpful nor meaningful to contemplate. However, with inputs from all directions and with the approval of all the parishes, we agreed to a name that seems reasonable to all concerned. The new joint benefice may be known as

'The Benefice of Lower Teesdale', because the Churches are on the lower side of River Tees and with the other group of Churches across the river in the Diocese of Durham were already known as 'the Upper Teesdale Churches'. I can say that it has been challenging, sometimes perplexing, but in all things God works through his purpose. I am able to affirm both the beauty and challenges of rural ministry in the light of the voiced concern about rural prejudice from some well-wishers, that over-all, the people of Teesdale, are warm and loving people.

Chapter Eight

A Shy Young Man

I could not forget how scared I was many months ago when I had a back-ache, after a fall on a slippery surface, and the implications of what this might mean. It was then I realised that my Last-Will which I have always prided myself to have perfected was actually not what I wanted. In the said Will, I simply divided my belongings, without a mere mention for my burial arrangements, which had become more relevant for the fact that I live away from all the conveniences and satisfaction of my cultural taste, being nearer my grave than I was 28 years ago. As a clergyman, I have officiated in as many funeral services in the burial of bodies, as in the Interment of Ashes or at the Crematorium. This awareness and the need to be considerate of others who will be saddled with my burial arrangements necessitated a re-think for burial plans. This persistent back pain had necessitated a visit to the Surgery and the doctor had recommended a blood test. There I waited like an expectant mother through a mental and psychological torture as to what the result of this comprehensive laboratory test would be. The insomnia I suffered the four days that I needed to wait between the test and meeting with my doctor was agonising for me. As a person who had been a regular guest in clinics and hospitals in Nigeria and Europe for close to twenty-seven years, I knew the risks which I had taken in the past from the acceptance of untested blood transfusions. At a time in Nigeria whenever anyone needed a blood transfusion, relatives or friends would either donate or get a person on a 'cash and donate' basis. With the benefit of laboratory hindsight today, only God knows how many infections have been so donated to the sick in the past. I looked back at my time in the barber shops, with many of the barbers then not knowing better hygiene discipline as we know now. But then, the barbers of my father's age were civilised. They ensured that they disinfected their shops and implements with kerosene or methylated spirit, but how effective that was I would not be able to say, but surely flies were kept away from those premises. My fear of blood test surely has to do with the fear of one's blood being infected through any shared blade or knife or the transfer of body fluid without precautions taken. Then my mind went to circumcision scenes. I cannot talk about my circumcision, because I was an infant when it was done. I know the man who did it for he came in for my junior brothers and my parents told me. He was a native doctor, and I watched him three times perform the operation for the little boys in my family. This native doctor had his instruments such as a pair of scissors, a knife, and a medium sized snail, all laid out on a clean piece of rag, the boy to be circumcised laid on a mat. This was all that was needed at his informal surgery. The surgery normally took place early in the morning, before the heat of the day but with enough light for everything to be seen without the need for the oil lamp. When the thing is done, the native doctor would break the shell of the snail and use its water to stop the bleeding. There was no bandaging, but a piece of feather was then used by the parent to drop palm oil or olive oil on the fresh wound on a regular basis to ensure that it heals in a proper manner. When it was the turn of my first son, it was done by a retired nurse in her clinic; I could no longer watch the scenario as I used to as a child, perhaps because things have changed. I stayed in my car till it was done. I could not afford to look at my son's face after the incident, because the boy was in pains. In my African home-town, female circumcision is not a practise known to us. But one evening, a family from the Middle-belt of Nigeria living in our town decided to circumcise a lady who was about to get married. Their belief was to prevent the lady from having a difficult child birth in later years and to keep her chaste. The lady in question was wailing and the boys were full of imaginations. We were young at about fifteen years old and this lady was about twenty, known to us, and we could not imagine why she was being so desecrated by the strange old people. After the incident, the community elders gathered together and invited this family to a meeting with an order that, such a practice must never happen again on our lands and they were forced to move away from the community. Surely, I shall be unhappy to know if any other person has been cut in this manner, because apart from being an abuse, it is definitely a form of pain and torture.

Expensive Sunlight

It was quite a big surprise after my medical test that the doctor, having checked the results of the laboratory tests looked at me and asked how I was coping with the weather. I told her that I was coping, after which she told me that I needed to be in the sun more, and prescribed eating eggs, milk, oily fish and other dairy products to supplement my lack of exposure to the sun. It was quite a relief that all my internal organs were in good state with low risk attached to them. Strangely, the doctor told me to eat more egg yolks and sun bathe more often as I needed it. That was a bit strange to me, and no wonder people from the very cold and Arctic regions flood the southern hemisphere for the sun. I could never imagine having spent a lot of years in the tropics for me to now lack vitamin D, and the need to get into the sun more often. When I was in Nigeria, the sun was probably my main source of vitamin D which was produced through exposure to ultraviolet rays. In sub-Sahara Africa, I was not deficient of vitamin D in the tropics, but strangely with all my boasting as the blackest man of my family, I needed to sun-bathe in the north ridings of the North-East England, where it was not unusual for the weather to be wintry even in June. It never dawned on me before that many of the white people who thronged to places they called 'exotic' in the southern hemisphere were in search of well—being and health. I therefore learnt to sun-bathe at the slightest opportunity. Sometimes, because sunny weather is not synonymous with atmospheric heat, I would stay behind my window glass or outside inside my car when the sun was out but the wind chilly, the glass would filter out the cold wind while I received the sun's radiation through the glass windows. The need for the sun which was an expensive item to come by in Teesdale encouraged me to buy a bicycle and to take more walks, having fun with window-shopping whenever I had the opportunity of a bright sunny day. For the rest of the year I decided to make friends with cod liver oil as my vitamin D supplement. To mark the second anniversary of my presence in Teesdale, God gave us the sunny spells right from the onset of spring, it was a stolen summer, and it came as a welcome development that I sun-bathed in my back-garden at the end of my second year in Teesdale. The anxiety generated by the test was also due partly to the fact that for some years I have been battling with high blood pressure and cholesterol, which seems to have abated in recent years but for which I was scared for genetic reasons. After leaving the Doctor's Surgery that day, I had a good night sleep, not that I sleep better when I am joyous, but that day I slept so well. Normally, whenever, I felt sad, or disturbed, at a drop of a pin, I would be sleepy, and would be ready for a nap whenever I experienced anger, but joy and happiness ironically keep me awake all night, thoughtful and anxious as to what it means to life.

A Trip To Bermuda

A whistle-stop trip to Bermuda set me thinking. On the approach to landing at the Airport, through the window, one takes in the beauty and notice white roof-tops on the island of Bermuda. Bermuda triangle had been made popular by the many stories which were not supported by scientific evidence, but which attracted me into a trip to America through the Island state. Most of their buildings have white capped roofs. I enjoyed the view of Bermuda group of islands so much that I wondered so much as to the beauty of Heaven. The white-capped roof tops certainly make Bermuda a unique Island and beauty to behold from the sky. Once I thought that if God so wished, it should be possible for humans to be allowed on holidays in heaven away from this riotous and turbulent earth, even if he would give an individual a maximum of a month every twenty years. Surely, I said, if the developed countries could issue visas, God could do more than that. Yes, God does more than that, for death remained our transition and the gateway for every individual but above all God has promised that whoever believes in His son, Jesus Christ shall have everlasting life with Him in heaven, John 3.16. The Bible left with us a description of Heaven with so many other details in the book of Revelation to our pleasant inspiration. No doubt heaven would be the utopia, as the place we all looked forward to be, where our God and our Christ Jesus would be with the beloved eternally till the end of time. But if God allows my wish for a holiday in heaven, how am I sure that there will not be the case of illegal immigrants in heaven, will the Angels be able to enforce compliance to conditions and permits as it happens today in our world? Absolutely ludicrous, as everyone who has faith in Christ while on earth has access to God as Father, citizens of Heaven, and Heaven will be home for us wherever we reside and as many as make it. At this moment my thought went to the great astronomers who first navigated the galaxy, especially Neil Armstrong, that great astronomer and how he would have felt almost fifty years ago when he walked on the moon. The strong souls of Armstrong and Gagarin and others beheld the moon on a temporary basis, and like the pioneers that they were, there were no facilities and infrastructure to lure them into an endless stay and they did not wait longer than was absolutely necessary, yet left a legacy that kept pulling the later generations after their trail. Even now that space tourism to the Moon and to Mars is being considered as a viable commercial enterprise and money being invested for the moon as a holiday place of novelty to spend a vacation. A vacation on the Moon and on Mars might seem unattractive today but, it reminds me of the time when my forebears went on pilgrimage to Mecca and Medina in Saudi Arabia from Ijebu Ode, Nigeria on foot. Later it was technology at work when my forebears came to Liverpool by boat from Lagos, Nigeria. This was many years ago before the introduction of more sophisticated technology that produced not only the bicycle, but the jumbo-jet and Ijebu Ode located in the tropical rain forest in sub-Sahara Africa was not privileged with camels. Some of the pilgrims to Mecca returned after three years while others never returned either because they settled along the way or because they did not survive their ordeal. Many years ago, when the first generation of Africans went to Europe and America to study, their relatives would escort them in large numbers to the seaport to bid them farewell, with many crying and sobbing because there was the possibility of never seeing such a person again. My parents and relatives cried out their eyes and hearts when Ademolu an elder brother left for Paris in 1975 and when I left for Yugoslavia in 1977, and no one was sure we would meet again. The reasons were many, many died overseas, many could not return for economic reasons or they simply chose to stay put in the comfortable country of their sojourn, many could not return because they did not find the Golden Fleece they came for and out of shame they would not want to become a disgrace to their family. While some whose relatives sold everything they had to send them overseas could not find the means to pay the debt back home and had sent their family into modern day bondage. Yet some committed an offence while overseas and the families concerned were living in shame in their community. There also might be some hang over of the slave trade in this, and to the fact that it was then understood that anything could happen on the rough turbulent seas, the African might meet with a spouse who might seduce their child from returning home, or that the allure overseas might not make their child to want to return. Worse still that they the parents might die thereby being denied the proper farewell without a funeral ceremony organised by their beloved child. The typical challenge will however remain the fact that the trip to Mars may require a stop-over for a long hazardous journey. The Moon might be a stop-over place, there will be the challenges of facilities and mode of financial transactions en-route. Already the African race is divided as to the benefits of the European incursion to Africa as proponents point to the level of literacy and facilities that the modern day African enjoys. The proponents are quick to point out that if the Europeans have not been to Africa, tribal wars and human sacrifice might still remain the norm, we could still be living in thatched-roofed huts, with no motor cars, schools and hospitals to mention just a few. However, the antagonists felt that both Islam and Christianity were alien to Africa and those civilisations which came with either religion also brought with them practices that were simply alien to us while denigrating ours, such as a way of dressing, respect for old age, and the value for our women folk among others. Others proffer that foreign religions actually helped the emasculation of the native people and that many people remain in one form of bondage or the other in the name of being religious. While some wondered that our old ways of building houses were ideal for our climate, and wonder what advantage the western education had if unemployment is the product of western education. As a fact I will boldly affirm that the African race benefitted immensely from western civilisation if the twin issues of corruption in the government service and colonial interest were isolated, as these make nonsense of many of the vantage gains. There is no doubt as can be seen from the modern day Africans in national and individual gains across the world that the world as a global village will always benefit from mutual interactions and understanding. I looked around me and realised that most of the indigenes of Bermuda are black people. Whatever brought them to occupy Bermuda as their country has ended up for their own good. The dispersion of the African race all over the world has helped the emancipation of the black race. Today there are no forced repatriations, people flee when the conditions are not conducive, struggle to keep their ground and return when the conditions are clement, as overcomers.

New York City to San Francisco

The last time I stayed in the iconic city of San Francisco, California, I had the honour of being driven round this cosmopolitan and one of America's iconic cities by Dr John a pioneer eye surgeon who drove my party which included my uncle and his wife around the city. I recollected some of my opinions of the places where I had visited like the 'Queen Vic' restaurant popular because the Queen of England dined there when she last came to San Francisco. I still hold a cherished memory of Stanford, and the University of California in San Francisco (UCSF), the wonderful Golden Gate Bridge connecting San Francisco with Oakland and Sausalito, a suburb of San Francisco, Redwood city and Oakland. It was a wonderful visit, but this time I was here on my own ticket unlike last time when my uncle footed the bills. This time I was wondering how much of America must have changed as I hoped to visit many places even though I refused to make cast iron plans as I would not like to be disappointed if any of my itinerary was not achieved. Meanwhile, it was intended that I would take a round—robin sort of trip either from NY city towards the north or from NY city to Gainesville, Florida along the east coast of America relaxing as much as my time and resources could accommodate. However whichever way I go, I intended to visit New Jersey heart foundation. This trip gave me the opportunity of visiting states such as—the state of New York, New Jersey, Virginia, and Philadelphia Cathedral, Delaware, Maryland, Washington and North Carolina. This trip was also for me a way to expunge from my system, the stress and anxiety of personal health which was confounded recently. Fortunately also, I have been to the west coast of the USA and to New York, but as developments might have changed some of the land-scape, and taking into considerations global security, I knew I must not loiter anywhere without taking my welfare into consideration. I had tried to contact friends such as Leke, my childhood friend and best man, now a professor in one of the leading American Universities whom I have not seen for ages and some of my ex-students in Nigeria who have become settled in the USA, and Mrs Oyemade whose prayerful support and her words of wisdom were of massive encouragement to my ministry. I wondered how much of sleep I would get as I intended not to stress myself but sleep, eat, walk round the cities window-shopping as every penny with me was budgeted. I also planned to visit the site of the World Trade Centre, the venue of the dastardly 9/11 act of terrorism in New York city, the Manhattan, Times Square, Rockefeller Centre, Wall street, and other land marks that gave New York her significance. The sight-seeing was planned to rejuvenate my sense of humour after the pain which my psyche has suffered. In New York and Richmond, Virginia and later in Raleigh, North Carolina I benefited from going to exhibitions and it was my visit to the centres of learning like the Universities and observing works of arts that did a miracle for me as these re-enacted in me the sense of mission and the vision to achieve my goals in life. I visited some Churches in Raleigh, Newark, New Jersey, Baltimore, Richmond, Philadelphia and New York and I felt the urge to go back to my congregations, charged to preach and minister the gospel. My visit to Raleigh to the Tim Soetan's family which was hugely coincidental stopped me from being able to visit all the people

I have planned to visit in the USA as we re-enacted all the fellowship we used to have when we were together in Belgrade, Serbia some twenty years ago. I was able to meet with John in Richmond, whom I have long years of contact with since he came as part of a missionary team to Osijek, Croatia and David, an ex-student of mine in the neighbouring state who also would rather wish that I stayed on a permanent basis in America. Tim, John and David were very warm and generous with their space and guidance, trying their best to see that I remained what originally endeared me to them. When I returned to New York, I was beaming with smiles and with a lot of my confidence regained, I got a direct flight from New York city to London. I heaved a sigh of relief as I returned to London.

New York City and down the East Coast

On leaving the JFK International Airport, New York, I made my way to the train station and simply followed my heart where to alight, it was rainy and the weather coupled with the thunder and lightning of that day was simply horrendous. The weather that day led to many cancellations to the trains, as many panicked during the rush-hour that day. I was not feeling comfortable on the underground train journey that evening, which was packed full of commuters returning from work, and I got off the train at a spot not far from Wall street and treated myself to a cold drink and a warm dinner. From there I picked a taxi that took me to the rail station from where I could board a train heading via New Jersey towards Raleigh in North Carolina. I took a particular train with connections that allowed me to satisfy my curiosity in cities and places of interest like Washington City and others along the route. I thought it was a good idea to start my tour this time from New York before gradually visiting friends and places in Maryland, South Carolina, Virginia, Ohio, Texas and Florida and spending my last week in New York, Chicago and New Jersey but I was wrong. I started visiting other places outside my original itinerary thereby not having enough time to combine the new and original programmes. In the varied and yet enterprising life of America, I was confronted by the sense of development in this vast country and their levels of expression of ideas with the massive media advertisement that seems to push things into the mind and sub-conscious of the individual. As a matter of sublime—sensitisation, I was gobsmacked when on a trip to Richmond, Virginia on a train journey to notice that police officers suddenly jumped on a train and started checking the identity of passengers. I was naturally shocked, because such occurrence would be seen as abnormal either in the UK, Nigeria or the Balkan states in the 1970s. Could this be as a result of the state of terrorism alert or what? Also within a month of this incident, there was panic when a water pipe busted with a loud bang on the street of New York City on a cool evening. Everyone including myself was alarmed and ran for cover. I quickly returned to the hotel where I was staying as I did not want to be found in a wrong place. The newspapers later that evening, recounting the events confirmed that it was not a terrorist attack but an old water pipe that bust and that the water pipes in the area were many decades old and due for replacement. It was a huge relief to know that was the cause of the explosion. This experience however, restricted my outings to Church services, and open-air sing-song affairs where I enjoyed a good measure of music, cold drinks and practice quietness of mind. My experience of not being a first timer in America was not actually helpful this time, because not only was the security terrain a bit challenging but the spiritual also. Normally, on vacations since 1991 when I was ordained as an Anglican clergy, I have made it a routine to visit and worship with other denominations at the slightest opportunity, in realisation that the Church is one and we are all parts of the same body. This time it was easier to make choices because of the divisions that were brewing within the ranks of The Episcopal Church. I visited many churches sharing fellowship and noting what concerns they faced, which is helpful in aligning the spiritual needs of the African and Christian souls that found a meeting point in me.

Chapter Nine

The Dead Rocked the Boat

Some of the issues that have slightly rocked the Church of Nigeria boat in my generation are the issues of polygamy in relation to the Eucharist and Mothers' Union, worship style and music, funeral rites for cult members and home burial. Apart from marriage and worship style, funeral services have thrown the Church into much confusion in the past and showed that the administration of the Church was short-sighted while chaos was raging. In fact everything about a funeral from wake-keeping, to the Church service and the reception after the burial have changed so much during my short life time and the way they have been handled has left a lasting impact on both the Church and society. Traditionally, before the advent of western civilisation, a dead person was buried according to common sense the second or the third day after the person stopped breathing. What probably seemed to be the major factor was if the dead person's children or the next of kin were present. Once it was becoming clear that somebody was in the final stages of life, the children would be sent for and it was always a great honour for one to bid his or her parents a final goodbye as the dying person said a final blessing on his or her children. Immediately the relatives present would then preserve the corpse using shear-butter to set the corpse in the proper lying-in state position while the body still had warmth. The family would now consult together with the children of the deceased at a meeting with the consent of the head of the deceased person's family but with the immediate younger sibling of the deceased person presiding. It was deemed inappropriate to find someone older than the deceased person taking an active role in the funeral, as they would be mourning, except for unavoidable situations. The Yoruba would traditionally want to bury their dead first, and on the seventh day after the burial expect the children of the deceased to prepare and distribute baked bean balls for the community, and a funeral reception would be held on the 40th day after the burial when food and palm-wine would be served depending on the wealth and generosity of the family of the deceased. After a reasonable time after the passing of an individual, the family would gather together again to distribute whatever property the deceased had left behind. This might involve where there were many wives and children, those to be cared for, who would be caring for the wives left behind and who would take care of particular children, either for their education or till they have learnt a trade and been equipped to practice such a trade. There was always a respect for the intention of the person who died which must have been made known to members of the family, and also for the fact that a half-brother or step relative could not possibly take over a wife of the deceased, this was to avert the possibility of people killing each other to snatch a beautiful wife. The Yoruba however found it difficult to inherit wives as this was a painful and sour point for those involved. Both for the new husband and the transferred wife, it often created a lot of tension within the marital home in which the woman suddenly found herself. The new partner could be castigated, or blackmailed and accused of killing the ex-husband if the new relationship became more complicated. As unfair as the system might be to the western mind or a Christian, it appeared that in the olden days it was the logical thing to do. This is because there was no social security, pension scheme or welfare system in place to take care of jobless young widows or fatherless children. The widows in this type of scenario always had the power of choice to accept what the family have proposed, or to reject the man as a new husband but might request that the man could continue to take care of her children. In this case she might wish to remain in her home; or she might have it mentioned either personally or through any of her relatives that she intended, after the mourning was over to remarry. What was not acceptable was for any male friend or new husband to be visiting her in her deceased husband's house. There were always input from relatives and members of the community to the cost of the funeral as many who are willing who attended give monetary gifts and other help to the children of the deceased to assist the funeral rites. The religious rites of mourning for the deceased however played a part as to what happened at the point of committal of the body to mother earth, because the Yoruba believe in life after death and that the deceased has only passed on from here to the here-after. On this issue of death and life-after, and in areas of respect for the elderly and child discipline, naming ceremony and marriage among others, there seemed to be least friction between the Jews and the Yoruba. One major attraction of Christianity when it was introduced was the Church cemetery, for its neatness and orderliness. The Yoruba traditionally bury their dead at home and when a house falls in ruins the landmarks of those buried there are often lost. On the platter of evangelism the issue of the secret cults taking over the committal in the Church cemetery arose, partly because the members were influential members of the society like high chiefs and legal officers, a battle line was drawn to determine who owned the burial grounds. First, the Bishops were not sure of their stand, some dioceses encouraged a funeral service to start from the Church and the Church would then hand over the important aspects of the committal to the family. They know well enough that the deceased was a member of a secret cult. At some point the Church would simply like a dog with her tail between her hind legs abdicate the service for others to take over. It was a period of multiple standards and the Church of Nigeria could not uniformly apply a single policy across the Province. There was chaos, and the priests could not even rely on the support of their Bishops as regulations were selectively applied. Unfortunately, the welfare of the mourners in the Nigerian Church appeared to be of no consequence, as not much thought was put into how they felt for the loss of their beloved ones, but the primordial fight over funeral rites became important. The bad-blood generated during this period in the Church of Nigeria was such a complete put-off even for me as a priest, as it was a period of lost opportunities for evangelism. Some people were put-off the Church of Nigeria by the way the issues were handled. For this reason along with other vaunted spiritual reasons, some left for either the indigenous churches, or rapidly helped the growth of the Pentecostal Churches while many people felt scandalised with the approach of the Anglican Church at that period. At that time, there were no places and time for the preaching of the Gospel but ideas that were only supported by the Jewish Old Testament being quoted out of context. Throughout that period the Church was missing a lot of the opportunities to preach the Gospel and created a terrible image for herself. The Church at that time was neither burying the dead, nor preaching the Gospel, but was busy fighting about the burial of the dead. For some time the Church leaders devoted all their time at Synods discussing how the dead should be buried, the Church herself fell into a coma, while some Church members became confused and bolted. But by the time it awakened from her slumber, there was a massive spiritual reawakening within the numbers left especially among the laity. Today as in many places, a Birthday thanksgiving service, funeral service or wedding may elicit a smile on the lips of a warden or Church treasurer as this means there will be many people in Church contributing to Church funds, and this may not always be welcome. It was gradually becoming fashionable within the Church to see a funeral service as an opportunity for Fund raising. I must confess my part in this as I also raised enormous amounts for the local parishes where I had served during the funeral or wedding services in the past. During this type of funeral service cum fund raising, it normally becomes a place of ego building by donors as relatives of the deceased outdo themselves. Today I will be tempted to call this act an abuse even though the practice in the Church of England ensures that for the funeral service, there is a fee for it and people who are willing can donate to either the Church funds or any charity of the choice of the family. That shall not make the Church ignore the dire needs of the mourners in the quest for Church funds. There are pastoral measures in place in the Church of England which ascertains the care of the bereaved families. Yes, the average Nigerian or Yoruba would love his or her funeral to be a celebration of some sort, with dancing, drinking and eating, with everyone present neatly dressed and happy, as many people do not wish for wailing and weeping at their funerals. They would love that everyone remembers their funeral for a good long time after their demise, as there might be 12hour partying and dancing with a live band in attendance immediately after the committal. Yet, that should not take away decency from the Church as Christians must remain the Light and a shining example to the world. Today, inputs such as type and choice of music and hymns, who took the readings or the allowing for the Eulogy in the funeral service in some Provinces, were only allowed for the burial of the powerful and mighty in the society. It was important for us to know that the deceased has escaped into another realm and beyond our judgement, and the bereaved whom we were to care for following the loss of their beloved ones are waiting to hear the comfortable words of Jesus and are not willing or able to be the recipients of their loved ones' judgement or convictions. Till today, the christening, wedding and funeral services remain lost opportunities if we shun those people with whom we would ordinarily have no contact except through these services. In the church of England it is important to plan the services with those on whose request the service was being made, arranging to ensure that there are no surprises in the service and to have the opportunity for pastoral care and counselling for the family, and to listen to their concerns in a non-judgemental way, expressing the love of Christ for all the world. About twenty years ago, when I was ordained, I could not have dreamt that there might be other forms of funeral service apart from Islamic and Christian, non-Christian but faith and traditional religious funeral services, for it was unimaginable that there could be other forms such as secular or humanist funeral services. Fair enough I have seen many other things that I would never have dreamt possible on earth, but it is releasing for me not only to know but to have witnessed these other rites, to enable me share the love and empathy of Christ with those friends who were bereaved. Recently, I attended a humanist funeral in the county of Durham. It was led by the junior brother to the deceased and included silence for people to pray if they "came from a faith tradition". The bulk of the service was taken up with tributes and reminders of the ways in which the lives of those present had touched that of the deceased. I thought that, if I had been a mourner of no particular faith, I might not have experienced this as a very satisfactory alternative to a Christian funeral. Attractive though it was, the humanist funeral contained nothing to show me where the soul departed was heading, perhaps it was heading nowhere, but that was not an option that I would choose for myself, as I am a child of God and I would love to return to him when my time is spent here on earth. Sometime, it was disturbing to find a large crowd of people in church who were not willing to respond to prayers or sing hymns. Yet as I grew in the Lord, I saw it as quite a privilege to have such a crowd even to hear the gospel being read and an opportunity for some meditation and share the Good News of Jesus Christ, and for people to know of the love of God. It is dangerous for the Church to see opportunities as threats, and we should always rejoice at the prospect of anyone getting the opportunity to listen to the Gospel even if this chance will cause discomfort to the way we do things. After all, the Church that lives to herself cannot be said to be different to any other club. However the Church is being run like a club-house in many places of the world as services such as christening or funeral or marriage are meant for registered members only. When a Church becomes a place for registered members only, there are problems and the issue of evangelism and Church need to be reviewed. The Scripture in 2 Timothy 4.4 warns us to desist from" *those who would turn our ears away from the truth to myth'*. I opine that a Church for all peoples has its risks, but Jesus himself took that risk when he dared die for all the world; '*for God so loved the world that He gave his one and only Son, that whoever believes in him shall not perish but have eternal life'(* John 3.16). The assumed challenge of the cultists and home burial in Nigeria nearly swept the Anglican Church off their feet. The popular secret cults that were known then were mostly the ones imported from Europe apart from the Reformed Ogboni Fraternity, a post-colonial society formed by the late Rev. Ogunbiyi who fought what he and some senior native, indigenous priests experienced as prejudice that were perpetrated by the white colonialists lay and clergy within the Church Missionary Society—led Church in Nigeria. During those dark days the legend was that the white priests felt it was derogatory for them to show deference and respect to indigenous African bishops or senior staff. Complaints and suggestions were rebuffed by the white European priests and some even had the effrontery to tell off the natives that the Church in Nigeria was an English Church and not African, which of course led to some moving from the church en block to form 'The African Church' denomination. At one point the church became so afraid of the extroverts while the civil-service models took over and this stood to the gain of the indigenous Churches. Ward 2011 further asserts that in the late 1880s a new group of enthusiastic CMS missionaries arrived. They were dismissive of Crowther's work and accused him of being a complete failure. This caused uproar within the Niger Anglican community. Crowther died at the end of 1891 and most of the extremist CMS missionaries left. CMS later apologised for the bad treatment of Crowther and the Niger Christian community. But they did not attempt to appoint another African diocesan bishop. James Johnson was promised to become a diocesan bishop, but he died while still a suffragan Bishop of the Niger Delta. The 1890s, was a time when the local Nigerian church, well established throughout Yoruba land since the 1840s, with a vocal presence in Lagos and with a strong if troubled existence on the Niger too since the 1860s, was at loggerheads with CMS. I should mention that, the Anglican Church made the Reformed Ogboni Fraternity and other groups popular among many people and took off any shred of secrecy from them turning them into a movement that began to go on parades on the major streets during the day time in a show of strength. My father was a member of the Reformed Ogboni Fraternity for many years and had reached the top echelon of his local organisation before he pulled out, long before all the rows within the Church of Nigeria. As he told us, his pulling out was due to the fact that my senior brother who was abroad needed funds for his education, he was not receiving any help from the organisation which he believed would support his son's education and later to give him a good job since most of their members were assumed to be leading professionals. The only person who sponsored his son's education was a Jehovah's Witness who was not happy to spend his money any further on a secret-cult man's son. My dad was left making a choice between remaining within the ROF and his son stopping his education abroad, or renouncing his membership after paying back entirely what he owed the fraternity. None of the choices was easy for my father even though he wanted to pull out, until one of his nephews came to his rescue and Dad was able to pull out of this organisation, by paying them everything he owed them. On a personal level, I was very disappointed with this organisation by a simple act of theirs. While I was in primary five, my father had needed to provide the menu for one of their meetings and that meant that food, a rice meal was prepared at home by my mother and I had to carry this load of rice on my head to their meeting hall, a distance of about a mile. Meanwhile, my mother for the fear of this society would not even taste the food while cooking as she believed that it was a taboo for non-members to taste the food of the group, and she cooked for close to two hours. Through the duration of the meeting, I was asked to stay with the steaming rice with my brother who brought the soup and meat. It was a nice, sweet flavour and aromatic environment as we waited under the tree in front of the ROF meeting hall with the cooked food. Later when they sent for their food, we were expecting to partake from the left-overs, but we were disappointed to find not a single grain of rice or any soup was left in any of the two unwashed bowls. It was with utmost dejection that we took home the bowls and a lasting impression was made about the secret societies from this event. Of course there were many assumptions and beliefs about the practices of the cults that were thought to be opposite to Christian beliefs and many people feared the cultists for different reasons, but my father would always warn that it serves no good for anyone to join a group that does not meet openly. What has caused the wide spread innuendoes about the secret societies to fester is because the public are not allowed to witness their meetings. This is where Christianity differ, the Church door is always open for anyone to enter and be part of our services without a burden of being part of the usual worshipping congregation, whether one is baptised or not, even though baptism remains our mark of initiation. The Anglican Church really helped the media publicity for this group, even though with evangelism in mind but by succeeding to drive away far from hearing distance those to whom the Church should have happily ministered. Other groups that were classified as secret societies then included some of the societies that those who have stayed overseas promoted after the exit of the Europeans who were the original brains behind them. Initially, those who belonged to these groups would have a commendation service in Church or the first part of the Funeral service and be refused a committal at the cemetery. Later there were arguments as to whether it was sufficient to bar them from the use of the cemetery or not to honour their funeral with any type of service. Churches from different dioceses made up their minds depending on what each diocesan Bishop or Synod agreed upon. The Nigerian factor soon helped the Church to settle the matter as many Church members move to defect to other denominations and some dioceses became jittery when rich and influential members of their Churches began to look beyond them and fraternising with other denominations; but the committed remained Anglicans.

Chapter Ten

Mission Implications

Within the old Yugoslav republics

In the Yugoslav republics including Serbia, Croatia and Slovenia, the impact of the communist rule and their version of 'self-management democracy' of Josip Broz Tito regime on the lives of the people went beyond political and socio-economic realms, for it affected their spirituality too. After the Second World War, many of the Church buildings apart from the government supported Serbian Orthodox Church convents and some Roman Catholic churches were either turned as museums or into other uses. The Evangel theology faculty building where I studied Christian theology was once a Jewish synagogue before the Second World War. The faculty simply added the Cross of Christ to stand alongside the Star of David on the pinnacle of the roof, but resisted any attempt to change the fabric or structure of the original edifice. Often the Yugoslavs would pride themselves as one of the founding leaders of the Non-Aligned Movement, that they were distinctively different from other types of socialism in the world. They struggled to balance the operations of their socialist economy with a free—market shaped democracy. One of the Yugoslav jokes during my time in Yugoslavia was that God abdicated their lands when they were being bombed during the wars. It was normal in those days however to look elsewhere, rather than go worship with priests who often cast for themselves an image of self-pity as they walked and dressed as people out of this world. They even have a peculiar way of speaking which was not attractive to me. During my return to Slovenia in 1988 and the situation after the 1991-1995 civil wars that broke up the Balkan state of Yugoslavia into constituent independent republics of Slovenia, Macedonia, Montenegro, Bosnia and Herzegovina, Croatia and Serbia, it was obvious that congregations now worship openly and in freedom. Josip Broz Tito, the Yugoslav war-time hero, nationalist, long-time president and legend, died in 1980, but left a legacy of bringing the constituents nations together as they fight the occupation forces during the world Wars. After his death, in order to pacify the restlessness of the nationalities, a collective presidency was adopted, where the six presidents seat together and a year at a time and in rotation, the president from each republic became the president of the presidency. The pending arrival of Buki in 1988 made me to go in search of the Church where we shall be worshipping in Ljubljana, Slovenia. I could not imagine Buki not attending a Church service on Sunday; hence a preparation for her welcome would not be complete without a place of worship. The search led me into the Evangelska Crkva (the Evangel Church) where Mihael Kuzmich was pastor. It was a hall in the basement with the pastor living on top. The Church eventually moved to a permanent place where more essential facilties were provided. At Evangel theology faculty, Osijek, Croatia through the hard work and commitment of Rev. Dr. Peter Kuzmic, Christian missionaries poured into Yugoslavia. They have a lot to challenge them for Yugoslavia was then a fertile mission field. At that time many Yugoslavs lived rough, into alcohol and many were impoverished. On a normal Sunday, people came in good numbers to the synagogue eager to know what happens in a Christian Church, and with desires for their hopes and life to be met by the gospel. The missionaries from different American Church denominations especially gave various support, establishing and building structures with their personal resources, preaching and teaching at every opportunity. The Bob and Sheryl Beard family were of particular support and all the students were grateful to them. The mission to the alcoholics and the street people were particularly helpful to our training as students. The various gifts from our generous friends in Croatia made it possible for us to support our family and some other immigrant families that lived in Osijek at that time. The Bible theology Institute established by the

Church in Osijek was established to train a core of pioneer pastors, an army of evangelists were being graduated and were commissioned with no churches to apply to for appointment but to go into all the corners of Yugoslavia to start new churches and ministries. Many received support from different overseas churches that spent huge amounts of money to support the pioneers to distribute Bibles, books and help teach skills. It is no surprise that today, the Christian Church has returned home throughout the emerging new republics with Evangel theology faculty, Bible theology Institute having played a leading role. This affirmed to other European States that it is still not too late to start again. However, with the religious freedom and wealth creation avenues, it is crucial that the Churches role in sound Biblical teachings and fellowship must remain the bedrock for Christian growth. It was great to see the Christians of Eastern Europe during the iron rule of communism learning by heart whole chapters of the Bible because it was illegal to have a Bible. Such commitments must not now be sacrificed on the altar of secularity and wealth acquisition.

Within the Church of Nigeria

Teaching and Fellowship

There is no doubt that the Churches in Africa contribute to the Global Church evangelisation and with prayers. It was glaring that if the route into finding an indigenous component have not been found through the establishment of the African Bethel Church and all the issues that enact the African traditional and religious worldview, there would not be a place for the African Christian to run into and return to challenge some ethos that could have destroyed the Church in Africa. I will dwell a little more on this. The Charismatic movement has had a particular appeal to Nigerians because they are closer in not alienating Christ from the God of the entire world, taking on board where the Africans stand spiritually.

Moreover, and more importantly, they did not try to alienate the African emotion from his spirituality. A good combination for Christian life in Africa will definitely include a Church where the Biblical teachings of the Pentecostal group are placed in the warm environment of the charismatic and socially receptive environment of the African indigenous churches. This combination is today found in many Anglican churches in Africa when other factors are isolated.

The Global South Anglican Agenda

Whatever is said about the Global South churches, they cannot in conscience be accused of keeping quiet while they need to speak out on the issues of human sexuality. At least, they left no one in doubt as to where they stand on the issue of homosexuality and same-sex marriage within the clergy. The strong leadership roles of many Anglican primates in the past such as retired Archbishops Desmond Tutu of Southern Africa and Jasper Akinola of Nigeria among others has created road maps in the Anglican Communion for strong Christian discipline. Their roles as trouble-shooters ensured that the way we do things must also be in the light of Scriptures and restrains each Christian to ponder on issues properly. Their teachings on ethics also help restrain the junta who would have ruled the nations with the proverbial iron rod. When priests with the spirit of prophecy say what the mind of God is on any issue, leaders bow and tremble. Today we need our leaders never to feel that the same–sex issue is the only major agenda. We can all see the effects of corruption on our everyday lives as we live in danger from assassins and armed-robbers day and night. Corruption, lack of infrastructural facilities, insecurity, gender abuse at work and in schools, poor budget implementation and abandoned government projects are major issues that confront the ordinary people on the streets and there is a strong need for the Church to give a good stewardship of their presence. The Christian Church must also clean its stables by ensuring that places where false doctrines and practices abide are exposed, that the Christian

Gospel must not be turned by anyone into a 'cash and carry basis' or give any space for occult practices or criminality.

The African and Christian Ethics

A casual visit to the major cities of the world especially into the western hemisphere will reveal the missionary zeal of the Africans and that they represent the blessing of diversity. Across the cities of New-York, London, Philadelphia, Paris, Bonn, Belgrade, Frankfurt, the African established churches are a beauty to behold and their evangelistic approaches quite attractive. They add something a little different to the spiritual landscapes of their hosts. I wonder what the lives of emigrants will be like if their types of worship have been entirely absent. However if all our spirituality can show is the multitudes dancing on Sundays without this reflecting on our everyday lives, what is that to Christ? The African Christians need to re-examine our morality and ethics. Where is the place of our presence if there is so much fighting, corruption, killings, forgery, gender abuse and other criminalities on our streets? Where is the balance between our faith and our religion? We need to practice whatever we believe God wants us to do, thereby leading others by our Christian examples and Africa will be better for it. No one wants the Anglican churches of the Global south to cross boundaries, but as their members are the vast majority who may probably cross their pastures; it may be advantageous for the Church to have counselling programmes that will help them remain stable under stressful circumstances. This can be helped if the members of churches who travel to the western world are introduced and encouraged to associate with any Bible believing Church for growth and spiritual nurture. Perhaps this will reduce the amount of bad publicity that emanates when any of our members is found to be with the wrong kind of a company or place at any given time.

Within the Church of England

The Swine Test

Barely a few months into my stay in Teesdale, a swine flu pandemic broke out in many parts of the world, first in Mexico and then gradually in Europe. The Archbishops' council at the recommendation of government doctors advised the suspension of the common cup at communion, and a non-tactile exchange of the peace during the pandemic in the United Kingdom. The question is who should decide what we do in Church? Reason, tradition and Scripture were the guiding standards of the Church, but how have we evaluated the medical recommendation in the light of Scripture? Should the way we receive the sacrament in the Church be guided by medical or quasi-governmental opinions alone? If the government can successfully press us on this aspect of our worship, how are we different to the churches in China and the old communist world that were monitored by their state? I am still wondering what the Archbishops Council would have recommended to the clergy if the Government had said to them, close the Churches and do not allow the people to gather together again. After all, they were able to stop us receiving wine and stopped us from shaking hands in Church at that time? If it does not matter, why did we not continue the method as a new Anglican way? Whereas the cinema did not stop operating at the time while people were still clinging onto the stands in the red buses in London and unto the underground tubes without anyone stopping the mass usage and crowding inside the London transport as at that time. If this approach to worship had been counselled and accepted in the churches of the southern hemisphere, the church there would have become extinct, yet despite all their health concerns and challenges, the churches in these places come out stronger. Was the Church so amenable as to drive herself out of existence? Were the buses, trains, parks and pubs more hygienic than our Churches that we could not shake hands during this same period? I strongly believed there were lessons for the Church of England to learn from this incident. After sometime we were informed through another pastoral letter from the Archbishops

Council that we could restore the chalice to the congregation after the swine-flu pandemic had proved to be more a panic than a pandemic though unfortunately some deaths were recorded due to it. This second letter also raised another fundamental question. If we have become like the others in using individual cups during communion, or giving the Eucharist in one kind by giving only the bread without actually drinking of wine, if that has been good enough, why go back to our old ways? If not, why did we do it at all? If care is not taken, Christianity may become a thing of the past in Europe at the rate of the present decline in the heartland of many countries. Many leaders want to hold Christian liberty with their fingertips while they heartily throw it away with their hands. It is becoming acceptable for Christians not to be able to witness, offer support and pray for their sick colleague or friend at work in the name of Christ in the guise of political correctness when other religions have a field day. Is it the good news of the Gospel that a lady was sacked from work for wearing a Christian cross, or a plumber for displaying a Christian cross were sanctioned, not in an Islamic country but in Christian Europe? Despite the quota and provisions of Christian ethics and morality for good governance, it appears that the old system is no longer sufficient for this generation. This is symbolised by the number of churches declared redundant or closed in the last ten years compared to any new churches being planted by the Church of England. If the multi-national corporations were to be managed like the Church in the past, many would have been sacked ten times over. The Church has so relied on family traditions and habits to maintain discipleship in the past that our evangelism and outreach now needs to be reviewed. Quoting Kostov 2009, a scholar who incorporates freedom of religion, conscience and speech as an observer and religious liberty advocate says 'any religious and ideological doctrine, which does not put its trust in the authentic Christ, sooner or later will resort to the power of government coercion, or totalitarianism, in order to realize its kingdom in the minds of people in the structures of society. Christian faith has a duty to stay away from any attempt to use public authorities to establish the principles of God's kingdom by compulsion'. This is the time for the national churches in Europe and the Church of England in particular to start again with enthusiastic prayers, Church growth, street and personal evangelism and the study of the Bible.

The Ministry of the City

What is the Church of England doing to support other nationalities in London? My journey of life in all probability is a testament to the resilience of the human spirit and the tenacity for which Nigerians are noted for and the Ijebu people in particular. The Africans have a saying, 'that if you get to any place under the sun and you cannot find a single Nigerian residing in the place, perhaps it is a place where no foreigner dares live'. Many hundreds of thousands of foreigners were abroad out of desperation and frustration, while many were out in search for the proverbial Golden Fleece or where the grass is greener. Many flee because what their parents used to call home has become for them a living hell, with violence changing faces at every second, and not a few were able to take a drop of their valuables with them into such exile. Listening to the chatting and telephone conversations which go on with most migrants on the red buses in London, one is tempted to wonder about the reason behind the fondness and great love the emigrants have for their mobile phones. This appears to be their last line of communication with the country which they have spent so much to escape from and from which they would be grossly sad if the communication were to be severed, because their relatives and loved ones are still in those countries of origin. Many of them were in menial jobs to keep body and soul together having stayed in the country, yet many were graduates of diverse disciplines which the corruption induced poverty from their country of origin had turned into destitute in a foreign country. One will be tempted to wonder where all the trillions and billions of money being budgeted annually by their home governments were diverted to. Every year there are budgets in many poor or underdeveloped countries for health and education and transport ministries to mention just three ministries. Yet over the years our general hospitals and schools receded into a shadow of themselves while the roads are virtually disappearing. The children of the corrupt leaders are living beyond their means in stinking opulence in the northern hemisphere, it is therefore a fertile ground for the Gospel, as the children of the poor, those who are struggling and the beneficiaries of corruption are rubbing shoulders in the mega-cities of the world. Where then is the role of the Church of England to serve and support these people? No wonder there is a multiplicity of Afro-Caribbean indigenous churches in London trying to minister whereas a good percentage of the immigrants from the Commonwealth countries are Anglicans by orientation who either swap pastures or become unchurched. Yet because of Anglican Communion guidelines it is not permitted for national churches to cross provincial boundaries. Who loses when the same ecclesiastical laws on boundaries do not relate to non-Anglican churches? One may be tempted to say that there are many Church of England places of worship, but there is something African in warmth, singing, dancing and praying that is absent which the African cherishes. For example, the Nigerian Christian will like to have a Thanksgiving for every success where it will be possible to dance to the Altar for prayers, or music and dancing for churching, birthdays and thanksgiving for the lives of parents recently departed this world. There is no doubt that the priests of the Church of England were busy ministers, who are involved with the Gospel for most of the time, with the demands of the parish. I can say emphatically that the work load for an average priest in the Church of England is far greater by any stretch of imagination than what five priests do in other lands. What about driving, administrative duties, accounting, liturgical and pastoral services. What is required for the creation of dioceses in some lands can be provided by many individual Leeds city Churches in the Diocese of Ripon and Leeds in terms of finance, transportation, housing, administrative support and clerical personnel. But if the black people and other ethnic minorities are to fully comprehend the role of the Church of England in a mega-city of London where they are a significant population, then the Church will need to review their operational strategy. I must affirm that I had enjoyed my time in all the places and countries where I had studied, worked and lived. St. Matthew's especially gave me an insight in preparing me for the challenges that confronted me in Teesdale. I was sad to leave London and the good people at St. Matthews, because some of the congregation had become for me like a family, and also I was leaving things that I have taken for granted in London into a life uncharted. When I came to England I was amazed to find that although the Church of Nigeria felt herself an exact copy of the Church of England this couldn't be further from the truth. In Nigeria the Church defends itself on the platform of Anglicanism, but on arriving in the UK I find that the Church of England has evolved and moved with the times, whereas the Church of Nigeria has remained steadfast in its ways just as it was when it was originally set up by the missionaries in Victorian times. The Church of Nigeria was not generally receptive to allow women in the chancel or as lay assistants to give the chalice during the Eucharist. I appointed one of the first female Church wardens in Ijebu diocese in 1995 at All Saints church, Igbeba, and there were some raised eye brows. I saw from the church constitution that officers should be communicants of a certain age who contribute to the church finance; no mention anywhere of the word male—female, and I did what was right. Perhaps, the Nigerian church, which fully embraced the 1662 Book of Common Prayer (BCP), need to know that the Church of England has moved on. Their liturgy is no more in the past even though those who cherished the 1662 BCP were not robbed of their heritage. Many leaders of the Nigerian church believe "Anglicanism", to be synonymous with the BCP, and I also found that the Church of England was a much misrepresented and misunderstood church outside Britain. Whether this is accidental or by design or sheer ignorance to cover some ineptitude by those concerned is left to be understood, however this could also be due to the English church method of communication with the outside world, in their mix-up of what was diplomatic or the indirect way of transporting views. With the level of changes in the life of the Church of England over the years, it is strange why many Anglican provinces have not noticed the changes. This statement might be shocking to express as the Church of England felt that they have always been there to see and know, but the laws in place have not made this realisable, as many priests and bishops from outside of Britain and the European Union have always had the chance to glance what happened but no opportunity to see, understand and know it. Without the latter, half-truth will continue to prevail in the Anglican world, about what the world believes the Church of England does or does not do.

Our Coping Skills

I. The Numbers

I recognised quite early the fact what my responsibility in Teesdale must be to see to Church growth, but at least ensure that the mission of the Church is accomplished. This of course is the role of the Church minister because a Church without the numbers is a struggling one. However, a Church building which is our own creation must not dictate the pace of what God can do or has done. The maintenance of historic Church buildings is a common burden which distracts from evangelism due to insufficient funds. How many we are, whether we are twelve or 70 or 244 or thousands matter but in as long as we stay on track with God's directions for our lives and ministry.

ii. Keeping Focus

It is also essential for me as a priest to ensure that I do not allow distractions to become major events. I must keep focus despite anything. Sometimes, the distractions are the by-products of my goals, but efforts are made to ensure that I do not major in the minor. And there are a lot of these. Any activity that does not compliment Church growth is out of tangent with my goal in ministry, and Church is not about building but God's children in his Kingdom. These involves; goals, release for ministry; engagement in acts of ministry. It is only when I am free to be engaged in ministry, walking along with someone or groups for Christ in ministry that the work is being done. Despite the challenges of ministry either on the spiritual or socio-economic platforms, and those things for which both the Diocese and I have no control on, we must remain committed to the task of evangelism. The cost of discipleship must never distract us from the focus of ministry.

iii. Praying Strategically

It is the task of the priest to pray strategically and work out the strategic evangelism and mission planning that can benefit Church growth. We all agree that the role of the Church minister is to be faithful, and Church will work out His purpose for God can use our diligence for maximum utilisation. The role of the Shepherd is to assist individuals within the parishes to discover their talents and to work out how enabling environments can be created for the actualisation of ministerial goals. I therefore set out in the search for mission partners within the parishes, those with whom we can achieve strategic objectives bearing in mind both their skills and their levels of communal acceptance and native intelligence, coupled with the faintest desire to serve the Lord. I started by giving all due encouragements and commending such types of personnel to God, supporting them through the process of growth in fellowship and the re-assurance of what God in Christ Jesus is doing through them among the people.

iv. Allowing The Spirit

In the light of manifested enthusiasm, there is a need to search and locate those who God would use to achieve his purpose. This is not with an intention of dictating to God but enabled by the guidance of the Holy Spirit to hunt for gifts and talents among the people. We are simply people who God uses through His Holy Spirit and must allow the Holy Spirit the control in the affairs of his world and Church. Discussions and the zeal of service make the possibility for success in this direction a reality. There are costs though certain obstacles that are products of human ego created occasional hindrances, but these are overcome through prayerful perseverance and humility..

v. Faithful Diligence

In diligence, we have nothing else achieved but to trust the Lord and steadfast fully commit to the task of mission even when there is nothing to cheer about and there are heavy clouds above us, yet it is important to trust He who has called us. During the ominous times when the zeal to pray tempts us to open the door and walk away, then the maxim is remembered, '*tough times do not last only tough men do*' or another still '*all these things shall pass away*". A trustful diligence keeps you going and I raise myself in such situations to remind myself of those before me who have passed through this way in much greater hardship or in sorrows but who at the end has won many souls for the Kingdom of God. After all, people of the world have their moment of sorrows, but one which does not culminate into joy may be a product of wasted moments. After all Jesus says, '*in this world there are many tribulations, but cheer up for you have overcome the world*'.

An Episcopal Style Of Multi-parish Ministry

Is there a conspiracy between the Laity and the priests to empty the Churches in the countryside by the celebration of the Eucharist every Sunday in the churches? I have noted within my limited experience that the Laity through the PCCs in many rural communities insists on Communion on Sundays to release them from responsibilities of involvement of leading services. The Eucharist ensures that a priest is present in Church. But with dwindling resources leading to a streamlining of priestly positions, with groups of parishes that used to have six or seven priests now being administered by just a priest, there seems for a need for a new thinking or at least a review of the way things are done in the Church of England. The Church of England does not probably start with the Eucharist as the only service every Sunday, indications from 1662 BCP show that the Morning and Evening prayer are said daily and this shows that they are the fundamental services. The Morning or the Evening prayer is a service that can be led by any Christian in the Church which keeps the

Church going, but there shall be willingness on the part of the Laity for this to happen. 2ndly, the way in which some Church buildings are structured with barely any provision for comfort/toiletries, time is a luxury that cannot be wasted. A straight Holy Communion service which does not give much room for in-depth study of the word is an escape route back to their homes. The few confirmed people who come to Church should not see the Church as a club house, even if it is a club, and then it should be a club of people who pursue the mission of Christ in their locality. On the other hand, having the Eucharist at every Sunday service enables the clergy to cling to the residue of available fleeting power and authority within the Church, while allowing them to get away with less. The Eucharist is at the centre of Christian worship is often the much-heard argument, but must we be taking the best meal every week to emphasise its importance? I make bold to say that the churches are deliberately disenfranchising the parishioners from having the opportunity to fellowship or encourage the people to worship. In a survey that I conducted within the parishes of Startforth with Brignall, Bowes, Laithkirk and Romaldkirk with Cotherstone in February 2010, it was established that while 98% of the respondents were baptised at the early part of their lives, only 18% of the respondents are confirmed. These days it is often difficult for parents to find confirmed persons to stand as god-parents for their children. Of course, confirmation cannot be forced on people; there is a clear need for the Church of England to start teaching again the catechism and biblical studies that can help the younger generation to have another go at evangelism. There are real and actual opportunities here as the Church is often in the unique position being the only one or among the few communal spots in the countryside which is the meeting point for residents in many locations; hence parishioners often want their Church to remain open even if no one attends to it. Churches with open churchyards are especially gifted because people seem to see it as their final resting place and subconsciously see it as theirs, but the churches with closed Church-yards will need to go step by challenging step. However, as the children grow older with upcoming wedding plans and concerns for the here and hereafter, this may help clear the mind of an individual as to the position of the Church building. I am of the opinion that the rate of decline must halt now, and the programmed fall or decline of Church congregation can be halted if certain steps are taken. 1. I am not for the laity presiding at the Eucharist; this may be as a result of cultural sensitisation since my childhood. I am not attempting to argue this theologically, but I am at the same time happy to see that the laity are released to minister in the Church according to the level of gifts which each has received from the Lord. My experience at the Diocese of Southwark while I assisted at St Matthew is refreshing here and how I pray that this can be adopted in the English countryside of Teesdale. There, at the communion table, the priest does those parts which are instructed to by the rubrics, while the laity takes all the other parts. This enables the Church to behave as one organism at the Eucharist and it is a beautiful way of saying, 'we are one body but with different parts' and there is often found many elements of the gifts of God enriching the service of Christ. A casual observation of ministry in our world today affirms that wherever the laity are allowed the full complement of their ministry, there is Church growth. Inhibiting the vast majority who has a vast opportunity of contacts will do the Church no good. The churches with strong growth in many countries of the world and in England do not always have the Eucharist as their principal worship every Sunday, but makes provision for the service. The Church of England already has in place a lot of formal and informal services that can be harnessed by the people if they are further encouraged. 2. Already, some congregations see themselves as the endangered generation, because of the quota of certain age-gaps within their fold and the lack of the younger generation groups in the countryside. Yes, the Church facilities in many churches of the country side are not children friendly and many adults go in there with some concerns for conveniences such as lack of toiletries. Since this issue has also become an excuse for non-performance, can the Church of England set aside some help no matter how minimal as an encouragement for churches to be community friendly? 3. I agree that the Churches of the countryside in the past has enjoyed a support in the middle-ages during the lead or coal mining generations and when farming was labour intensive. Today, it is easy to hear from the farmers how difficult it is for them to leave milking or cattle-rearing or how erratic weather can make a mess of their programme if time is not duly honoured. I have also observed that farming associations are closely knit together. The level of solidarity between farmers, especially at the funeral of a farmer is enormous. Farmers would be found standing and chatting long before and after such services, and such discussions are for the trained initiated ears as such bantering are often couched in the special vocabulary of the farming communities. For this reason it is not a surprise that the farming communities show great enthusiasm in the services such as the Plough or the Harvest services and to funeral services as this point to death and resurrection as a parallel from planting and harvesting. In the training of clergy and ministers, at our Colleges of theology and seminaries, it is very crucial that the specific of farmers be included in the curriculum. 4. The Scriptures place the Lord's Supper at the centre of worship (Acts 2:42; 20:7; 1 Cor. 11:20, 33), and not as an appendage or an occasional extra; therefore it is important to remind ourselves that Holy Scripture places the Lord's Supper at the centre of Christian worship. Jesus did not intend it to be regarded as an option. It is the soul and heart of the New Testament worship. In fact, His Supper is the very foundation of the New Testament, for Jesus instituted the New Testament by giving us this sacrament. Jesus said, *"This cup is the new Testament in my blood, which is poured out for you" (Lk 22:20)*. So we see that the Lord has given His church both the Word [which we are to publicly read and preach (Rev. 1:3; 1 Cor 1:18)] and the Sacrament of the Altar which are to be administered whenever we gather in His name (Lk. 22:19-20; 1 Cor. 11:23-26)]. Following the outpouring of the Holy Spirit on the church at Pentecost, the Christians *"devoted themselves to the apostles' teaching and to the fellowship, to the breaking of bread and to prayer" (Acts 2:42)*. The first Christians' worship looked remarkably similar to ours in basic structure. It included God's Word (the living voice of Jesus), the offering (*koinonia* in the sense of "sharing in something"—the hands of Jesus in action), the Sacrament of the Altar (the living Jesus Himself, according to both His human and divine natures), and prayer to the living Lord in their presence. This reflects the daily worship of the first Jerusalem church. Later St. Paul, on the mission field of Macedonia, followed the same practice of offering both Word and sacrament to the believers (Acts

20:7; 1 Cor. 11:20, 33). This type of weekly Sunday worship, which always included both the Word and the Lord's Supper, was universally observed even before any books of the New Testament were written. Paul reflects this weekly Sunday communion practice in 1 Corinthians 11, noting that Holy Communion is the very reason they are meeting in the first place. *"When you meet together" (v 20)*. Hence "In the New Testament, the sacrament was a regular and major feature of congregational worship. According to Schoessow 1997, Holy Communion continued to be the chief Sunday Service in all major churches of East and West throughout the entire history of Christendom to the early 16th century, citing the Didache, an early Christian document dated as early as A.D. 50-70 says, "On the Lord's Day, His special day, come together and break bread and give thanks." By the time of the middle ages things had deteriorated and in an attempt to remedy the deteriorating piety of its people the church in 1215 the council ruled that all Christians *must* commune at least once a year. This was the condition of the Roman church at the time of reformation. I am in no way demanding that people must reduce their level of communion. Each person is free to partake of the communion weekly if this is desirable and in good conscience to commune, but those different churches within a benefice give the people the choice to be either part of an informal service, Eucharist, Morning prayer, Evening prayer a straight Bible study. The sacrament is there, and if a Christian desires to receive the Lord's gift, it is available. Therefore, there may arise a need for a format that incorporates the episcopal type of multi-parish ministry in the countryside, that enables our lay members take more active liturgical roles while allowing the clergy concentrate more on pastoral and sacramental roles. This of course will need the full support of the Bishops who will need to convene more local conferences and speak at more vestry meetings to gather the support for and encourage more laity participation.

Chapter Eleven

The Anglican Covenant

—After The Ink Dries—

There are worldwide forty-four autonomous Churches that fellowship within the Anglican Communion. Each is autonomous and general assumptions are hard to make because there is no single Anglican Church with universal juridical authority as each national or regional church has full autonomy. The Church of Nigeria for example is a membership Church, and you may have to subscribe by an annual payment and participate by church attendance before you are recognised as a member of the Church whereas The Church of England is open to everyone. A casual observation shows that one of the greatest flavours of the Anglican Communion is that we do things differently in different cultures. The Anglican Communion has no formal structures, but the three or four Instruments that hold the Communion together are:—Lambeth Conference—this is an occasional meeting; The Anglican Consultative Council (ACC); The Primates Meeting and finally the Archbishop of Canterbury. The Archbishop of Canterbury is the head of the Communion but leads by consensus, a position assigned by the fact of history. He is one among equals at the Primates Meeting, without the power to discipline. It is left to be seen how effectively the issue of discipline is taken up after the Covenant is agreed upon by all. The Communion is presently under stress due to innovations from some Provinces which others see as sacrileges in the house of God. The issue of women ordination and consecration is one that polarise the Church, while many Provinces are for it and have gone for it, many others felt they are not ready for it as yet. The other issue is the rising profile of homosexuality in the northern hemisphere, and the role of the Church in its adoption. Many Provinces of the southern hemisphere especially in Africa are vehemently against homosexuality and not in least among the clergy or its tolerance within the Church. The consecration of gay bishop in the Episcopal Church of United States of America in 2003 seem to have been the straw that broke the camel's back, and the confusion that sets from that time is yet to abate. According to GAFCON 2008, Akinola's paper titled "A most agonising journey towards Lambeth 2008" states that *'in February 1997 in Kuala Lumpur during the 2nd Encounter of the Global South Anglican Communion that a statement was issued expressing concern about the apparent setting aside of Biblical teachings by some provinces and dioceses'*. He stated further that *'in February 2007, the Primates of the Anglican Communion met in Dar es Salaam, Tanzania as they tried to repair the Communion that had been so badly broken'*. At this meeting they gave those whom they believed have brought the Communion to the brink of a break-up seven months to reconsider their actions. Akinola then asserted that *'the leadership of The Episcopal Church USA (ECUSA) and the Anglican Church of Canada (ACoC) seem to have concluded that the Bible is no longer authoritative in many areas of human experience especially those of salvation and sexuality'*. The Global Anglican Future Conference (GAFCON) was formed in December 2007. Akinola also quoted that even *'during 2004 there was a growing number of blessings of same-sex union by American and Canadian priests even though the Windsor Report released in September 2004 reaffirmed Lambeth resolution 1.10, and the authority of Scripture as being central to Anglican Communion life'*. GAFCON 2008, quoting Okoh, then the chairman of GAFCON Theological Resource team and presently the Primate of the Church of Nigeria, agreed with Akinola in explaining *how 'in recent years, huge amount of time, energy and money have been expended, in search for an agreeable solution to the human sexuality controversy in the Anglican Communion. It has remained elusive'*. Okoh concluded *'that the issue at stake was much wider than the human sexuality concerning same-sex unions. What had been is the challenge to the authority of the Bible in all matters of faith and practice'*. An attempt to bring the house to an orderly quiet and reconvene, with the goal to regulate the method of introducing new practices within the Communion is leading to the introduction of a Covenant. The Covenant will in essence mean that Provinces shall need to consult widely, seeking consensus, before introducing new practices. The idea of The Anglican Covenant is excellent but worrisome is the implementation of a code of practice. If the Archbishop of Canterbury who presides over the Anglican Communion is one among equals without any power to discipline, how does he effects sanction? Already, the Archbishop is being accused of inaction, or incapable to discipline and maintain orders which may not be in his powers to perform. Is anyone thinking of transforming the informal structure of the Communion through the Covenant into a power structure? This may be unacceptable to many other Provinces. Meanwhile when a Province is interested in a power structure which is against the tradition of another, where and how are the opposing views of structure and discipline within the Communion going to meet? Up till now and despite all our imperfections and I am yet to see a perfect organisation, the Anglican Communion seems to have acted like the soul and the eye of the world. The eye cannot see itself except through a mirror but others see it clearly and it can see others. It is dangerous for the eye to be sick. Both the Churches in the global north and the global south have experienced difficulties in dealings with each other. Sometimes the Churches of the Global south feel concerned and experience frustrations with understanding the mechanism for decision making or felt betrayed by approaches or liberty which to them have not been washed by the word of God. Again many Churches of the Global North may ask themselves where the Churches stand in the Global South when Government and public officials siphoned nation's wealth and yet remained untouchable community leaders. Being part of the Anglican Communion has advantages but it comes with a responsibility. There is always the need for understanding the mechanism of dealing with and interpreting the human expressions of the other people. There is also the challenge of believing that the Anglican Communion is a Church of 'via media' only in tradition and liturgy. That will be a great risk indeed, if allowance is not made for dynamic and rising cultural expressiveness, ethos, and the effects of scientific breakthrough which enrich the life of the Church universally. Being part of the Anglican

Communion helps me realise, that I am a part of a massive body and this enables me to share and moderate my views on issues that used to confound me. It is a fact of past and present history and hopefully for the future that the Anglican Communion by initiating global evangelism from the 1830s into the Global south, despite human imperfections, created peace and love without which wars and human suffering would be on a more massive scale. Even if being part of the Anglican Communion is seen by the business minded as a form of 'Franchise', it is a franchise that should continue to give the world and the universal Church, an Agenda for stability. This is in spite of the situation in which we are now, we need to look at ourselves again from the mirror of the Gospel, and take a stand for mission, holiness, unity and pray to walk more closely with our LORD Jesus Christ. With the acceptance in principle of the Church of England that clergy in Civil Partnerships, or in other words Same-Sex relationship, can be bishops provided it is a celibate union is simply open to more questions. Such questions may include, 'how do you decide or know what happens behind the bedrooms of people concerned? But is this the time for a witch-hunt? When a bedroom is closed, unless you are a party, it is closed to those outside it, but remains open to the ever-seeing eye of God who shall judge everyone at the end of the world. I am convinced that it is not possible to include all the details we shall need into the Covenant at this time. I am aware that what applies as fashionable in or acceptable in Asia may not be welcome in Europe and what Africans see as reasonable may be unacceptable to the Americans, therefore there shall definitely be rooms for cultural manoeuvre within Provinces. The Covenant should give each Province the opportunity of listening to another opinion about their ideas, provided the review may encourage a modification that will receive a general appeal based on Christian morality, ethics and spirituality. My third concern about having a common document that will take care of the tensions in the Anglican Communion by way of a Covenant is on the issue of effective communication. This is because the manner of communicating in English language between England and the rest of the world is not uniform. The English speak and use their language as a tool of diplomacy either for business or leisure, but that is not how the rest of the world communicates in the language. The English use words such as: perhaps, may be, probably, hopefully for the things they want done or desire, but this is not a positive statement for many other people of the world. I was not surprised when I heard from two of the Provinces of the Global South that the language of the Covenant is not clear enough. Even if the Covenant is to be signed up to by all the Provinces, the ingredients for disharmony and tensions are already inherently carved into the document. But I shall wish that the Covenant is supported by the whole council of the Provinces of the world as this will be a platform for further discussions as to stop communicating would spell the death knell for the Anglican Communion, an organisation through which the Christian Church has benefitted the world greatly. The atmosphere of the Church and the environment which the Anglican Communion was creating for the humanity which was its duty to evangelise, alongside the seeds of disharmony and prejudice being dug and heaped upwards is a matter of grave concern. I assume it is easier to feel strongly about a speck in the eyes of a neighbour and ignoring the log of wood in yours, while wallowing in ignorance and maintaining a comic role in the society. Of course, when religious organisations or their leaders begin to gloat in the ridicule, indignity, and condemnations they impute to others, then the world cannot but wonder where our sense of religiosity lies. Many people provoked strong feeling, but shall we not be concerned when strong feelings of righteousness tip over into loathing? If our hatred makes us feel good inside, we can be sure that something unpleasant is going on. I suspect that because of the nature of communication in the northern churches, and the placement of huge emphasis on non-verbal cues, those who dialogue with them might simply have been listening to their own voices and then take the silence from the north as a means of victory for their arguments. But no, the Europeans are their own masters and they know how to keep their counsel if a discussion is degenerating into a shouting match. There are fears among many national Churches that our diversity as a Church may become hampered in the future, leading to an over-regulated, fear-driven Church. This fear is shared by so many people including myself. The beauty of the commitment we all share in Anglicanism today is borne out of our freely chosen adoption of worship style while trusting that we shall continue to remain brothers and sisters of the same faith by doctrinal values. Our rich formality of informal structures without powers of enforcement safeguards the guarantee of a free association without undue hegemony and structures. Scruton 2011, in his treatise wrote ' *the virtue of the Anglican Church is that it is neither clearly Protestant nor clearly Catholic. Many people (including myself) argue that the Anglican Church is not only a compromise in itself, but a place in which compromises can be worked out and agreed upon*'. I want to minister to the whole Church with a voice, tenacity and temperament of an African and the guided quietness and resilience from my enlightenment, together with the necessary understanding of both. It is perhaps time for all of us to listen to our voices and examine if what we are hearing is what we intend to say, or mean to say. It is time to review if our speech is of Jesus' style, if he is to mount our local Church pulpit today. The psycho-religious diatribe going on between the northern and the southern Provinces must not be allowed to get too divisive. The level of threats of separation or dissolution of communion is another form of spiritual violence that were not heard of even in 325 AD when the council of Nicaea was called to solve extant church problems or the council before it with the first set of disciples in Jerusalem. I feel there is a need for a review as to what causes the feelings of anger or betrayal felt by the southern Provinces. Part of the problem might have been the spread of religiosity without a proper hermeneutics in cultural context. The Churches of the south should not make villains of their Christian brethren in their quest to exercise spiritual freedom of choice. There are of course personality problems which might be a difficult issue to admit as a lot of energy has been released. The reality of the Christian in the southern Provinces is that of a fighter (a Christian soldier) who battles 'Satan' and his angels, even if this Satan is in the cultural or a theological creation. Generally, Christianity in the southern Provinces is about power, which power dominates and which is superior. In worship, sermons, singing and in prayer life, the southern Christians dwell on the power of Jesus, of God being superior to Satanic and human power. They are involved in the fight between darkness and Light and Christ being the Light of the world and having all authority on earth and in Heaven to deal with the enemies mean a lot to most Africans. They understand the world's 'darkness' as the Jews of old might understand it, even though darkness is not totally a negative thing. Darkness allows the glory of light to be appreciated for it might be indicative of gloom but more than that it might indicate depth, treading carefully and the power of the unknown. Maybe energies may be better diverted to evangelism in sharing with the world what God expects from humans rather than dwelling on the negative. This will make evangelism become an instrument of peace rather than the art of polarisation and self-righteousness. It is absurd and regrettable that some Provinces have not created the time and the opportunity to discuss issues that ultimately affect them regarding the Covenant because the leadership has a fear for a proper discourse. The discussions in some provinces are between what the leadership felt right to say or think instead of having a meaningful discussion of the contents in their Synods, which ought to include the diocesan and deanery levels. About five hundred years ago when Henry VIII married Catherine of Aragon, the first of his six wives the Christian world started on a journey. This was the period when sexuality of the clergy became controversial. The Church was at the centre of most villages and towns, and the idea of the parish church representing the life of the entire neighbourhood was to be expected. Life in England and through most of the western Christendom during the time of Henry was regulated by the traditions of the Church and its celibate priesthood. When the king married his sixth wife in 1543, the Reformation was under way, and among the priests were clergy with wives and families. There had been married priests in the early church, but from the third century constant attempts were made to enforce celibacy without much success, but this led to many abuses. Those who supported clergy marriage were those who were favourably disposed to the reformation, as the clergy wives had been considered as concubines and their children as bastards. It was challenging for a lady to consider marrying a priest as it was derogatory or of superb courage for women. At that time, women were considered to lack morals, if associated with a priest, even a Bishop. The clergy more or less then have to find a private space to keep their wives and families away from the public eye to avoid the harassment involved. The annoyance caused the King by the sermons and teachings of Martin Luther in 1539 made him deprive the English clergy their privileges in the benefices' and, some were threatened with death, unless they agreed to permanently separate from their families. The clergy however enjoyed some moments of respite when Henry died in 1547, and Edward VI who ruled after him reversed his decisions on these matters, allowing those already banished to return to England and legalising the marriage of priests. However, on the ascension of Mary, clergy marriage was again made illegal and clergy were made to divorce their wives and separate from their families if they were to enjoy their benefices or they were made to relinquish the holy orders. For a long time in the history of the church, these problems caused a lot of division and discomfort within the rank and file of the clergy and it was not until the time of James I and VI after the plea of the clergy was the marriage and children of clergy made legitimate. On the other hand the issue of sexuality even as diverse as the situation in Henry viii's time moved full swing from the issues of five hundred years ago to year 2003 events with the consecration of a gay priest as bishop. Are we dealing with the same types of situation now? Both enforced celibacy and homosexuality along with polygamy, infidelity and others confront Christians with spiritual concerns (1 Timothy 4.3; Romans 1.18f). There are not many issues that divide the world, but the issue of homosexuality and ordination of gay priests as Bishops was simply a catalyst that manifested the break-down in communication. Years before polygamous relationships in African emerging Churches and gender issues were on the front burners of division in the Church. The Church of England was vehemently and adamant against polygamy because it was not patterned on Christian spirituality. The western world till this time is against polygamy. They can dare do the same with other sexual challenges including homosexuality. The Bible in the book of Leviticus, and in Paul's letter to the Romans showed us some things as an abomination and concerns raised on such issues such as: problems, idolatry, roof-top design, and talks about the diagnosis and cure of various ailments by priests, women being unclean during menstruation, and the eating of certain animals which do not part the hoof and chew the cud among others. We can all as well look at this list of abominations, and stop being selective, if we can.

All Sexual Sins will Be Equally Sinful

The provinces of the southern and northern hemisphere may be humble enough to examine our mindlessness, and be able to see what the blood of Jesus has done for us at Calvary. The Scripture do not want us to cover our transgressions before the Lord, but to confess and forsake them and be forgiven. A born-again Christian would be disgusted to find out that the seventh commandment. "Thou shall not commit adultery' (Exodus 20: 14) was not enforced for all sexes as it applied only to married women. Examples abound, for example, Reuben (Gen. 35:22) Judah (Gen 38: 1-24), Samson (Judges 16:1 l), David (2 Sam. ll:1-5) among others, committed the sin of adultery and were not put to death. Surely, Reuben and David were punished while Samson lost his freedom and life, for the Scripture says 'no sinner shall go unpunished'. Whenever a married man was involved in sexual relations with a spinster or a prostitute, it was not counted as adultery against his wife. If on the other hand, a girl engaged to be married to a man, or a married woman had sexual intercourse with anyone except her husband it was counted as adultery and the lady and her partner were liable to be put to death (Deut. 22:22-24). Defining adultery as a sin against the husband was not peculiar to the Jews. The situation was also the same as the legal traditions of the ancient Rome, and the Yoruba of Nigeria. With this definition of adultery, a woman is seen as the exclusive property of her husband, but the man is free to contract as many marriages as possible. In the Old Testament times polygamy was not the norm, rather it was the exception because of the high marriage bride price (Genesis 24:22, 53). Among the Yoruba of Nigeria, a man may turn polygamous with the aim of making his wife jealous. However, a man having an extra-marital sexual relationship with a single woman is tolerated. The woman is usually known as a 'friend' and if the woman bore a child for the man, the relationship continued for a long time, the woman is treated with greater respect and as a wife, a member of the family. The woman is expected to be faithful to the man and be responsible to the extended family with all her children legitimised by the man's claim. The 1979 Constitution, however, gave legal backing to such children for no child in Nigeria can now legally be called a bastard for the man is expected to care for the child and mother as he does to his legal wife and her children. But the practical implication of this relationship even though marriage by co-habitation is recognised as part of the culture of polygamy yet this other wife does not have, and will not be accorded, a high personal integrity as the legal wife. The Nigerian law does not permit second marriage without dissolving the first, otherwise the culprit will be charged with bigamy. The only way one can be polygamous is through marriage contracted under native law and custom. But the truth is, many second marriages are contracted through co-habitation, but the practice is socially acceptable, but is sometimes frowned upon. Depending on which Church denomination one attends and the conviction of the minister, this is sometimes tolerated by the church. Such a wife will need to remain faithful to the man and his family for her position to be recognised but without the level of security and status of the married wife, therefore such a wife depends on her own skills. Many years ago, people who did not share a common view on sexuality were not tolerated, until it became apparent that spiritual giants and family for whom we have great respects might not be straight. The presence of a door or key for our bedrooms is indicative that we should not allow the personal to destroy the collective. With God, sin is sin, even though people will prefer to classify the sin of others as mortal. I am one of the Anglicans in this world who do not believe that physical suffering is always as a result of sin. Yes, there are infectious diseases, and diseases caused by our habits or way of life. I knew to believe that would be to condemn all people who were suffering from malaria through mosquito; the effects of robbery, rape, drought, tropical rain storm, flood, earthquake or tsunami as consequences for sin. The Anglican Communion is based on mutual trust and respect, and that should remain the basis of our Covenant, not in any legalistic fashion. No matter how strong our fellowship today, there are bound to be incidents that may question our sincerity in the future which will need resolution based on respect and the loving relationship that we have for each other. The human mind is a developing one as God challenges us and opens our eyes to new things in our lives. God showed Albert Einstein, Galileo, Nikola Tesla and our Church fathers in different parts of the world what he did not show the rest of the world, and this was called invention, insight and wisdom. Shall we in the future have to wait for the rest of the world to catch the glimpse of a vision before we advance? Where then shall be the position of our civilisation in the 24th century? Have we forgotten that at no time in history were inventions made without challenges from a group who felt God would be offended? How do we then solve the problem of depravity of the human mind? Often we are faced with the misuse of invention that can lead to destruction such as the pursuit of atomic bomb instead of nuclear reactor for electricity generation, which of course may have sinful intent. The truth is if we have stopped any irregular movement, not even the reactor for the electricity, computer, telephone, motor car, or the aeroplane will be in place today. Yes, The Bible says, 1 John 3.6 'No one who lives in Christ keeps sinning' while Hebrews 10.26 says 'If we deliberately keep on sinning after we have received the knowledge of the truth, no sacrifice for sins is left, but only a fearful expectation of judgement'. We must all know that we *cannot continue to dwell in sin and ask grace to abound'* but we all need to re-examine our faith and the contents of that faith. Whenever any smaller group of people uses threat to severance of relationship from the rest of their larger group, it displays the inability of reason and the paucity of positive arguments. If this is coupled with the concern to challenge our faith in Jesus Christ who though sinless came to dialogue, dine and die for us—*'For while we were still sinners, Christ died for us' (Romans 5.8),* then we must review our stand. Still on the issue of same-sex relationships, the Primates of the Global south believe they are helping Jesus Christ to cleanse the temple, while the Primates of the northern Provinces believe God had created everyone as a unique human being with both sides believing they have given all to find a lasting solution. If God created everyone so uniquely, could he have created the murderer, armed robber, rapist and others of those types? If he did, why condemn their habits, even though God loves everyone, some may be tempted to ask? Have we as a Church stopped believing in pastoral care? If one shouted too loud, he might not hear when a helper calls. On the other hand, if one keeps too silent expecting to hear his name called even when it sounded like a drop of pin, he might not realise his situation until he is fast asleep. The danger therefore is not only in the listening, it remains also in the ability to hear when the solution appears, given by the Spirit and received through the Spirit of God. The arguments of the past has not given reasonable reflection to those that differ on the issues of sexuality, be it homosexual, heterosexual, polygamy or celibacy. To many Christians, sexuality defines one's adherence to Scripture and determines who can be called a Christian. The debate since 2003 has too often highlighted the negative, while the church neglected to preach Christ crucified and risen. Matt 28 ask us to go into the world to witness, yet our wrangling seems to be achieving the very opposite as each group castigates the other to prove who can win the argument. In the current argument, the European Church drew the first blood when they insisted in the past that polygamists should be prevented access to the Eucharist in the young and emerging Church in colonial Africa and that Africans should send away their wives except the first one. Even though homosexuality and polygamy may not be in the same group biblically, they both share the same psycho-sexual influence on human actions. In the early 1900 when the Church of Nigeria was about to take shape, the Anglican authorities opined that polygamists could not share the Cup of grace at the Holy Communion, which was a matter of concern to many Anglican Nigerians especially the Yoruba people who were then predominantly polygamists and other tribes who were converts from Islam. The issue of polygamists partly led to the formation of African Bethel and other African founded churches. The mishandling of the polygamy issue by the early emerging Church in Ijebuland created massive opportunities for Islam and enabled the great Balogun Kuku to become a Muslim. This is partly responsible for the major gains of Islam in Ijebu Ode and the environs because Balogun Kuku had a large followership. Later a surge of people relocated into the indigenous Churches like the Cherubim and Seraphim church movements of the 1920s and 1930s but the vast majority stayed back and opposed the notion. They kept quiet and silently ignored that provision in their constitution which otherwise would have led to the decimation of the Anglican Church in Nigeria. The Africans saw polygamy as cultural and necessary for their well-being but the European Church saw it as sinful. There are many other assumptions with doubtful theological credibility and no proper doctrinal foundations that were fostered on the Africans by the missionaries in the past.

Is this an issue of retaliation?

Is homosexuality being used by both sides to fight both homophobia and gynophobia? It appears that African Anglicans have an inordinate fear of women. Among the Yoruba male chauvinism is still actively present even though many of the traditional religions have one form or the other of female leadership. In many Churches in the Yoruba heartland, licensed women Readers are treated with a level of prejudice or at best second-rated. They are in many places prevented from entering the sanctuary during worship and have to stop at the chancel railings at the offertory. The first ordination of women in the Church of Nigeria took place in 1993 by Bishop Haruna of Kwara diocese. This ordination created an excitement in the life of the national Church, and the ordination met with hostility and was heavily criticised by the House of Bishops. When Haruna retired two years later, the Church of Nigeria disrobed the three women. My understanding was that the ordination was as confounding as it was welcome depending on the perspectives of many Nigerians, but casual observations confirmed that Churches where women were allowed to take active ministerial roles even in Nigeria flourish more than Churches that inhibit and exhibit sexual and gender prejudice towards women. What could be responsible for the ban on the ordination of women priests even though African Church leaders mingle freely with women ministers and founders of other Christian denominations? This appears to be flagrant gender discrimination and it needs a rethink. Without much ado, if the Global south have not achieved a sexual 'el-dorado' or chastity within their ranks, the attention to the northern hemisphere may seem diversionary. I am convinced that the majority of Africans see the sexuality debate as blight on their Christian heritage, a major distraction from spirituality and a laughing stock of other religions in Africa. No! Their priority is about surviving victoriously over all the forces of darkness from within and without. We seem to be actually putting ourselves into a prison of our own theological assumptions beyond which peaceful coexistence is difficult, and this should never happen between peoples of different faith, let alone believers of the same faith whatever the denominations. The Church of

England is the mother Church of the Anglican Communion and for the House of Bishops to keep silent when they could have doused the flames with previous opportunities may not have served their purpose. There are lessons to be learnt for the future. The old English proverb says '*A stitch in time saves nine*'. Perhaps the skill to stitch timely was not without concerns. It is a bit quiet for us as Christians that since the 2005 statement on civil-partnerships and despite all the arguments both nationally and within the Anglican Communion, the House of Bishops in the Church of England has not published further statement that is in the public domain. Thornton 2011, says '*the then Archbishop of Canterbury and later Lord Runcie (1980-1991), commissioned the national church to examine the situation of urban poverty in England which in 1985 brought about a report titled 'Faith in the City' which was seen by many as a direct attack on Thatcher's economic policies*'. There is a need for the Church of England to work out again their lasting principles. I am also convinced that the Gospel is clear on what God expects from us, and this puts the overall teaching of Christ into the equation, shall mean an honest relationship between the husband and wife. What needs to be further defined is who a wife or husband is? Even in heterosexual relationships, it is not always clear when the husband may not be the man, or when the lady of the house occupies the marital role of the husband. Can we examine ourselves without hypocrisy and weed off anyone who has fornicated either now or previously, take off the list every adulterer, anyone who has looked at any woman or man with lust and had a thought that was carnal, or anyone who has benefited from a polygamous or homosexual relationship, or anyone whose virginity was in doubt at marriage or who married anyone who was not chaste before marriage and within marriage. Yes, this proposition is potentially dangerous, as a Bishop who has been involved with any sexual sin may not be able to effectively uphold the sanctity expected of his office. Any Christian who is perfect, without sexual stain should be on the Register of those to be elected into the bishopric. If the sexual past is taken into consideration, or what some do behind their closed doors, perhaps they ought never to have been appointed into the lofty offices they hold. Therefore, it may be considered as something that is christianly to look at the present faces of our leaders to see if any of them are willing to confess their past sins and be saved and this would be the person expected to tell other sinners what Christ Jesus has done in his or her life. It amuses me when I notice how much damage self-righteousness has done within the Christian Church. Are we interested to know how Jesus dealt with the past sins of all his apostles, sexually or otherwise before asking them to follow him? I recognise the fact that Jesus started his ministry and like John the Baptist asked those to be saved to repent of their sins, which suggest to us that people repent of sin as a condition for their being saved as the Lord till today wants us all to repent and be saved also. Many Church leaders would rather see others rot in hell so that they can be vindicated, rather than in heaven, but our task is to increase Kingdom citizens for Heaven, by loving actions bringing others into the saving faith which is obtained by believing in Jesus Christ. Those God calls into the Church ministry may not be those who have never touched sin, but those who recognise what they have been and repent. There is a huge anxiety and concern from others when Christians and Church leaders are glamorising their sins and sinfulness, not least when such persons are occupying exalted positions of trust. I also assume that some Church leaders will rather want others to confess their sins to them and not to God, or put themselves at par with God to determine who is forgiven or not. The hearts that are yearning to serve the Lord must not be suppressed by human instincts and flawed morality, till we become as a church where no souls are saved any further.

Despite All These

What shall be the basis for continuing communion between Christian Churches across the world despite our sexual views? Is it realisable to expect all national Churches to inform others where they stand on all issues that are cultural red-flags? This will be absolutely impossible if the Holy Spirit is to be allowed a space to work and act among his Church. In the affirmation of the Scriptures, we must realise like Paul that on this side of the divide be it global north or south, God will be our ultimate judge. Instead of judging each other, let us ponder Christ crucified for our sins and Christ risen for our justification. Neither gender nor sex is the problem, but as human beings forgiven of our numerous sins by God through Christ. Let us put our diversities aside and focus on one thing that *'while we were yet sinners, Christ died for us'*; that will be where the future lies and that is our task in evangelism even when that has led in the past to the upkeep of public morality and decency. We must avoid any regulating that will put the Church permanently into a civil service frame of structures. Love and trust must remain the bed-rock of Anglican discipline without hoisting a government on the Church. This is not with an intention to say to anyone to become reckless and allow sinfulness to abound. No! According to Romans 6.2 'We died to sin, how can we live in it any longer?' The creation of super structures can only increase the burden on those to superintend it when it is glaring the said officers will lack powers to discipline, for anything to the contrary will be removing the basic freedom that our Anglicanism is based upon, which is the sovereignty of each province. The amazing Gospel developed from Judea to Galilee and in Matt. 28 verse 19 Jesus asks us to go to the entire world, and in Mark 16 he emphasises the need to preach to all creatures. In today's Church we can balance the aims for the world evangelisation in contrast to the schemes polarising the Anglican Communion into global north and south. The question shall be whose interest are we hoping to serve? Christ's or our own. *'Among you there must not be even a hint of sexual immorality, or of any kind of impurity, or of greed, because these are improper for God's holy people.'* (Eph. 5 :3). In other words Paul the apostle is saying that sexual immorality must not happen among us, whatever the type, content and style. Paul further warns us in 2 Cor.5.10 *'For we must all appear before the judgement seat of Christ, that each one may receive the things done in the body . . . . whether good or bad'*. He mentions the testing of our work in Eph. 6.8 *'you know that the LORD will reward everyone for whatever good he does'*. Our expected reward from the Lord will then be in proportion to our service and will be based on our obedience and faithfulness to God and his instructions in the Scriptures. The Gospel according to Luke 19.11-26 shows us that our level of compliance will determine our heavenly reward and responsibility for the future. Paul concludes in 1 Cor.3 12f 'if any man builds on this foundation using gold, silver, costly stones, wood, hay or straw, his work will be shown for what it is, because the Day will bring it to light. It will be revealed with fire; and the fire will test the quality of each man's work. If what he has built survives, he will receive his reward'. These statements from Paul the apostle does not mean that sexual matters, especially those counted as trespasses should not be discussed but that it should not arise from us. The on-going arguments and becoming a signatory to the Anglican Covenant must not lead us to Church Provinces that will in the future be afraid to take bold steps for the Gospel. The greatest problem for the future lies in the fear of antagonism from other Provinces that may not share the innovative ideas of another, if the innovation is seen as sinful. Of what use to the Gospel in our world is a Bishop who will be afraid to hurt a fly, even though the work of the Gospel is not to hurt people but to enable access the Throne of Grace. The Church has always had different opinions and differences be it theological or pastoral. Whatever the impact of that, the future will tell. There is a beauty in the context of our spiritual relationship of simply being present in the lives of the people as friends, sharing the anxiety of the people among whom we share the same humanity. We need to share our hope and love in God with each other as we pray for each other. What is the place of prayer in our common life if all we can give to another person going through crisis is criticism and self-righteousness? Some may ask, is gloating in sin, a crisis to be empathised? The answer is we need to pray for all sorts of peoples, and peoples in diverse conditions. That is part of our ministry and all peoples include Christians, non-christians, leaders, followers, atheists and all manners of people. Shall it not be a false sense of victory if we allow the negative spirit to fix a wedge of division and disintegration into the Christian Church in the name of being a better Christian than the other? The Scripture has presented us with strong images that enable us contemplate walking together as a united, loving, affectionate and yet independently minded children of God. In Mark 1.16 *Jesus was led by the Holy Spirit of God into the wilderness . . . .* '. Are we already wishing our world to be mono-cultured, where Christian spirituality rooted in morality and ethics abide, a place for those who think, believe particular things or act in ways that will be acceptable to general norms? Will that be said to be part of the end time signs? If your prayer is to be led by the Holy Spirit of God, would you have prayed that you will be led into the company of wild beasts of this world, whatever that means? Therefore, part of the situation when we are being led by the Spirit of God will entail that we are humble to learn what God teaches daily in our relationships and interactions and be at peace with all men, for our LORD Jesus is the Prince of peace. This Shepherd continues on his journey. Shalom.

Definition Of Terms

Alma mater:—It is the school, college, or university at which one has studied and from which one has graduated.

Agemo festival:—Agemo, a traditional masquerade of Ijebu people, is believed to come to town with other deities after three days of traditional rituals during the festival and women are forbidden from sighting the Agemo.

Anglican Communion:—is an association of national and regional Anglican Churches in full communion with the Church of England and specifically with its principal primate, the Archbishop of Canterbury.

Criminal Records Bureau (C.R.B) :—is a statutory organ in charge of vetting all potential personnel who would be working in close contact with children and vulnerable adults in the U.K. This is to ensure that abusers and other criminals were not given another opportunity to abuse.

Oro festival:—Oro is a cult of the collective ancestors which confine women indoors when they have tasks to perform. Such duties include public sacrifices, executive meetings and execution of condemned criminals or banishing trouble-makers. It is a cult with collective responsibility as no single individual is responsible for their actions.

Ijebu:—The Ijebu People inhabit the South-Central part of Yorubaland. There are immigration legends which tend to link the Ijebu with the biblical Jebusites and Noah (hence Omoluwabi—omo ti Noah bi—the children of Noah) but these is yet to be proved.

Italupe:—This is the place where christian Gospel was first preached in Ijebuland. The first Church sited on the place is St. Saviour's Church now moved to Italowajoda. The second Church established on the site is Emmanuel Church. Ita-lu-pe means the place from where the Lord is ringing the Bell or from where the Lord is calling. The Bell donated by the missionaries is still in use.

Lambeth Conference:—The Conference of all Bishops of the Anglican Communion held every ten years. It used to hold at the Lambeth Palace but it is now held at the University of Kent in Canterbury.

Kabiyesi, Oba Alaayeluwa:—This is the title of a paramount ruler like Awujale of Ijebuland which can be equivalent to His Royal Majesty. He owns the land and superintends the affairs of all the Oba of the land. The Oba Alaayeluwa used to hold supreme power and authority in his territory.

Oba, Kabiyeesi:—Oba in Yoruba translates to King in English. Whereas there is His Royal Highness in England, the Yoruba has Ka-bi-e-ko-si, written briefly as Kabiyesi which means a person beyond query.

Primates:—All the 38 provinces of the Anglican Communion has a Primate each who is the Archbishop and metropolitan or the Presiding Bishop, with six other independent churches.

Primates' Meeting:—This meeting was established in 1978 and it is one of the instruments of the Communion. The 1998 Lambeth Conference strengthened this instrument. To GAFCON, it appears it is not living up to expectation.

Province—Each country consisting of all the dioceses or small provinces make up a Province.

Sub-Sahara Africa:—The countries south of the Sahara desert in West Africa.

The Anglican Consultative Conference (ACC):—The ACC was established in 1968 to facilitate the work of the Churches of the Anglican Communion. It coordinates actions and exchange information as it maintains the structure that enables the Communion fulfils her mission to the world. Every province has at least a member on the Council.

Venerable:—A title for an Anglican Archdeacon.

Vestry meeting:—An annual meeting of the Church congregation to discuss any item of interest and to receive the reports from the Parochial Church Council and other information that help the mission of the local Church.

Yoruba;—The **Yoruba people** (*Yorùbá* in Yoruba) are one of the largest ethnic groups in West Africa. The majority of the Yoruba speak the Yoruba language (*èdèe Yorùbá*). The Yoruba are spread throughout West Africa, especially in south western Nigeria and substantially in the Republic of Benin, Barbados and Togo with large groups of Yoruba migrants living in the United States, Brazil, and the United Kingdom. They are found predominantly in Nigeria and make up over 21% of its population.

References

Adesanya, S. A. (1997). The effect of extra marital affairs to the family instability in S.W. Nigeria. Unpublished M.Ed. dissertation. Ogun State University. Ago-lwoye, Nigeria

Adesanya, S.A. 1998. The Caring God. Danky Christian publications.

Adesanya, S. A. (2000). The Sexes under God. ljebu-Ode: Danky Christian Publications.

Adesanya, S.A. (2002). Correlates of Marital stability among couples in South Western Nigeria. A Doctor of Philosophy thesis. University of Ado Ekiti. Nov. 2002.

Adesanya, S.A. (2005). Marriage is a nest not net

Ajibola, S. (2011), WFI Report on Malaria. Nigeria

Antil, J. K. (1983). Sex role complementarily versus similarity in married couples. Journal of Personality and Social Psychology.45, 145-155.

Brochure, (2000)—Oba Sikiru Kayode Adetona, The Awujale of Ijebuland's 40th Coronation Anniversary Brochure.

Church of England: *anglicancommunion.org/*

Colins, G. (1992). Christian counseling: A comprehensive Guide. London: Laster company.

Cutright (1971). Income and family events: Marital stability. Journal of marriage and family 33 (5) 291—192.

Ellis, B. J. (1992). The evolution of sexual attraction: Evaluative mechanisms in women. New York: Oxford University Press. pp. 267—288.

GAFCON, 2008. The Way, the Truth and the Life'—Theological Resources for a Pilgrimage to a Global Anglican Future. Prepared by the Theological Team of GAFCON. The Latimer Trust. London

Johnson, Samuel: History of the Yorubas, London 1921

Kalu,U. 2011—In Just Human—A commentary on How childtrafficking network operates in South East. 30 July. Vanguard Newspaper. Nigeria

Kostov, V. 2009—Christian Mission in Post-Communism:Missiological Implications and the Bulgarian context. Christianity Today. Bulgaria

Parcevall Hall—A booklet produced by the warden of Parcevall Hall advertising the facilities available on the premises

Pincus F. L. and Ehrlich, H. J. (Eds). (1999). Race and conflict: contending views on Prejudice, Discrimination and Ethno violence. Boulder, co: West view L. C.

Osborne, D. 2004—The country vicar.—Darton, Longman and Todd Ltd.—London.

Otokiti, S. 2011 Churches everywhere yet immorality abounds. Nigeria Compass. 28 August 2011.

Reyment, R.A. 1965—Aspects of the Geology of Nigeria. Ibadan. University press. 145

Runcie, R. 1985—Faith in the City—Commission that authored it was established by and acted in the name of Archbishop Runcie.

Russ, W. 1924—The Phosphate deposits of Abeokuta province. Bulletin of the Geographic Survey of Nigeria. N. 7

Scruton, R. 2011—Christians—The Anglican Communion. The Times.

Sedmak, M. (2001). Auto Biographical Approaches to studying Ethnically Mixed Marriages. Socialno Delo. 40 (2-4), 181 ff.

The Ijebu people:—www.ijebuassociation.org/history.htm

Thornton, Ed, 2011—'Archbishops are consistently political', Church Times. No. 7735, 17 July 2011 quoting a report—'Turbulent Priests? The Archbishop of Canterbury in contemporary English politics' by Daniel Gover. Theos.

Ward, K. 2011—'In Kevin's correspondences with Stephen'. 4th October 2011.

Wikipedia—the free encyclopedia. Henry Townsend (missionary)

Printed in Great Britain
by Amazon.co.uk, Ltd.,
Marston Gate.